"Trying to overcome the power of sin by simply observing the command-ments of Scripture is hopeless. Dr. Wakefield shows how the grace of God operating through our new life in Christ sets us free from the power of sin. I strongly encourage you to read this book and discover how you can live a liberated life in Christ."

DR. NEIL T. ANDERSON, AUTHOR OF *THE BONDAGE BREAKER*

"Norm Wakefield gives us the nails to close the coffin containing sin's domination over our lives. As a mental health professional, I can strongly and gratefully endorse this book for those who are tired of trying to achieve 'victory over sin' through self-discipline and willpower. Dr. Wakefield gives good counsel to both the individual believer and the church community."

DR. GLORIA GABLER, MARRIAGE AND FAMILY THERAPIST

WHO GIVES A R.I.P. ABOUT SIN?

breaking sin's death grip on your life

DR. NORM WAKEFIELD

IVP

InterVarsity Press
Downers Grove, Illinois

InterVarsity Press
P.O. Box 1400, Downers Grove, IL 60515-1426
World Wide Web: www.ivpress.com
E-mail: mail@ivpress.com

InterVarsity Press® is the book-publishing division of InterVarsity Christian Fellowship/USA®, a
student movement active on campus at hundreds of universities, colleges and schools of nursing in
the United States of America, and a member movement of the International Fellowship of Evangelical
Students. For information about local and regional activities, write Public Relations Dept.,
InterVarsity Christian Fellowship/USA, 6400 Schroeder Rd., P.O. Box 7895, Madison, WI
53707-7895, or visit the IVCF website at <www.ivcf.org>.

All Scripture quotations, unless otherwise indicated, are taken from the Holy Bible, New
International Version®. NIV®. Copyright ©1973, 1978, 1984 by International Bible Society. Used by
permission of Zondervan Publishing House. All rights reserved.

Cover photograph: Tom Maday/Photonica
Cover design: Design Concepts

ISBN 0-8308-2310-7

Printed in the United States of America ∞

Library of Congress Cataloging-in-Publication Data

Wakefield, Norm.
  Who gives a R.I.P. about sin?: breaking sin's
death grip on your life / Norm Wakefield.
    p. cm.
Includes bibliographical references.
  ISBN 0-8308-2310-7 (pbk.: alk. paper)
  1. Sin. I. Title.
  BV4625 .W35 2002
  241'.4—dc21
                                                                        2002004135

P	17	16	15	14	13	12	11	10	9	8	7	6	5	4	3	2	1
Y	15	14	13	12	11	10	09	08	07	06	05	04	03	02			

To Jody and Jeanie Humber,

two dear friends
who have encouraged and
supported me in this venture.

Your lives have enriched countless people.

CONTENTS

ACKNOWLEDGMENTS

I've written a number of books and know how many people make direct and indirect contributions. I appreciate those in the Faith Friends Community who listened to my teaching and affirmed and critiqued much of the material for this book. I am indebted to people over the past years who have helped me sort out bits and pieces of truth in my own journey toward spiritual wholeness.

I am thankful to others who have contributed to my writing process. My wife, Winnie, has been my best critic and proofreader. When she says, "Honey, it's not clear," I know it's not clear! She has an eagle eye for catching my misspelled words and typographical errors. I also value the comments that Gerald Sanchez, Jody Humber and Cremin Benson made as they read through the manuscript. They sharpened my thinking with their kind and perceptive comments. And I found the insights of Cindy Bunch and her team invaluable. My heartfelt thanks to all of them.

I am especially grateful to our Lord Jesus Christ for the mighty work he accomplished on the cross that delivered you and me from the penalty and power of sin. In the days when I felt defeated by the power of sin, I always found myself turning to his love, forgiveness and instruction. He gave me hope and motivation to move forward. Thank you, my beloved Sovereign!

INTRODUCTION

One of Leonardo da Vinci's greatest works of art is *The Last Supper*. When he began working on it, he asked Pietri, a young man who sang in the Milan Cathedral, to sit as Christ. After he finished painting Christ, Leonardo continued with the other characters, spending twenty-five years on the painting. Finally the only person left to complete the memorable scene was Judas Iscariot. The painter sought to find the right person to represent Christ's betrayer. One day as Leonardo was walking on the streets of Rome, he spotted a sinister-looking character who he felt would convey the image of Judas.

The man agreed to sit for Leonardo's painting, and the work began. As he began to survey the painter's studio, old memories began to surface in his mind. He remembered an image from when he was a young man. When the image became clear, he spoke to Leonardo: "Maestro, I was in this studio twenty-five years ago. I then sat for Christ."[1]

When I read about this incident, I was left with a feeling of sadness. It also drove home the subtle, destructive power that sin has to ruin a person's life and lead him or her down a pathway of evil, despair and hopelessness. Not everyone becomes a Pietri, but all of us feel the persistent voice of sin enticing us to go in the opposite direction of all that Jesus Christ represents. I have lived the greater part of my earthly life and can attest that the power of sin has left its mark on me. And as one who has been a pastor, counselor and seminary professor, I have spent hours with individuals who are trying to resist sin's power or are grieving over what sin had done to them or those around them.

You have in your hands a book that represents my study of the Word of God, what I have learned from others and my own prayerful ponderings. It came about as others encouraged me to put into print insights that they felt have helped them in their spiritual journeys.

You may wonder why I've chosen the title *Who Gives a R.I.P. About Sin*. The question "Who gives a rip?" often suggests that people don't care. My experience is that people do "give a rip" about sin in their lives but don't know what to do to overcome its persistent control over them. The R.I.P. is meant to be a play on the idea "rest in peace." It reminds us that sin robs us of a fulfilling life, and for many it leads to death.

My prayer is that this book will be both instructive and encouraging to you as you seek to walk with our Lord Jesus Christ and live a life free from sin's vicious and destructive power.

1

THE REAL
PANDORA'S BOX

"I think I'm the world's worst goof up.
I love the Lord, but I'm always doing the wrong thing.
God must get real fed up with me."
"MAX"

"Create in me a pure heart, O God,
and renew a steadfast spirit within me."
PSALM 51:10

I've known David since my early teenage years. Before I met him, I'd heard others speak of him with admiration and tell me I should get to know him. After I'd met him, I soon loved to listen to him speak. And the more I heard him speak, the more I was attracted to him. His love for his Lord was deep, rich and intimate.

Then one day I noticed that pain seemed to be seeping from every pore of his body; it was woven into the fabric of his words. He had done something awful, and the fruit of his unrestrained passion was crushing him with grief. He was left with tainted memories that would haunt him for years. His family and friends would feel its impact. His community would know it. And because of his high stature, the world would know it.

"Oh, my Lord," he sobbed, "how can you stand me after

what I've done? Oh, my God, how desperately I need to know
that you still love me. But I find myself wondering how you
can after the way I've violated and hurt others. I yearn to be
cleansed from my sin. I want so desperately to find freedom
from the condemnation that plagues my mind. I've abused others. I've failed my family.

"But you're the one I've really failed," he continued. "You're
the one I've betrayed. I've always told others how compassionate and mighty you are, yet I didn't heed your counsel, and
now I've sinned against you. I've cast shame on your name. My
stupid, self-serving lusts violated all that you hold dear. You
have a right to whip me, to judge me, to condemn me. Your
actions are justified, whatever they may be. Please have mercy
on me. Please be compassionate."

You may think that I've been reviewing a brokenhearted
confession of a defeated Christian who came to me for counsel. But instead I've shared what I hear in the agonizing confession of one of the most revered Old Testament saints, King
David. In Psalm 51 this man, beloved by his Lord, expresses
great agony over the adulterous sin he committed in the heat
of misguided passion and over the subsequent murder of the
woman's husband, a man devoted to David and the nation he
served.

Sin is a destructive power that cheats, robs and kills the
guilty and innocent alike. It whispers in our soul's ear, telling
us we deserve the forbidden fruit that will bring us pleasure
and fulfillment. Like Novocain, it numbs our brain so we function on pure passion. But in the end, we discover that we've
played the fool and are left with a stinking cesspool in our
soul. Though we look at David's sordid episode and lament,
"How foolish. How could he commit such a wicked act?" deep
in our hearts we know that we have been hewn from the same

tree and are capable of the same evil.

We all fall victim to sin. We see this reality in ourselves and in those around us. Tina would agree. She had a mother who was too busy and a dad who had been taught that warmth and affection were signs of weakness. Tina was left with an insatiable longing to be loved and cherished. Then a young stud promised to fulfill her need—in the back seat of his car. Tina got pregnant, and the man sped away to find another victim.

We'd like to think that this teenager learned a lesson, but a couple of years later she got pregnant again. The longing for love and affection hadn't gone away. The last I heard of Tina was that her life was spiraling downward with shame, defeat and loneliness.

Would you be surprised if I told you that Tina was an active teenager in the church I attended? I don't doubt that she had committed her life to Jesus Christ and wanted to serve him. But her hunger for intimacy was intense, and no one helped her find a valid way to satisfy it. I believe that she prayed like King David and felt the pain of her sin. In my conversations with her, it was obvious that she felt humiliation and felt she'd failed her Lord. But Tina had no understanding of how to defend herself against sin's power, so it raped her again and again.

I could make a long list of Tinas, and Todds, Toms, Tillys and Torrys, whom I've known who genuinely trusted that the work of Jesus Christ on the cross paid for their sins. But they were powerless in the face of sin's subtle, relentless seduction. All of them had been caught up in passion that promised to satisfy their inner hunger. But in the end they had been swindled.

There's Becky, whose knack for biting sarcasm has left a trail of wounded people behind her. She's been deceived into thinking that her clever putdowns mask her own sense of inferiority. Elliott sins against his wife and young children by working long hours to feed his fear of failure. Ying cheats on her college exams because she's scared to death of disappointing her parents. Bart jokes about his eating binges, even though inwardly he hates himself for them. In their moments of honesty, they would admit that they are often troubled by the patterns of sin and its consequences in their lives. Their sins may not be what our society considers big sins, but they are enslaving, and they rob them of the joy that comes from intimacy with our heavenly Father.

By the way, my own name is on that sin list too. I came to faith in Jesus Christ when I was twelve years old. When I prayed to receive him as the covering for my sins, I thought that heaven would open and I'd become a purified, victorious Christian. How quickly I discovered that sin never took a holiday in my life. In fact, I was more troubled by sin after Christ found me, because I knew it was an offense to my Lord and a violation of all he stood for. But I couldn't find a strategy or technique to deliver me from its persistent clutches. I'm reminded of a cartoon by Mary Chambers that I once saw of a small group Bible study. In it a lady says, "I haven't actually died to sin, but I did feel faint one time."

A long search. In my early twenties, I applied to Moody Bible Institute to study the Bible and become better equipped to serve my Lord. I sat through theology classes, listened to "victorious Christian living" sermons at Moody Memorial Church and read books about dealing with sin. Though I was earnestly seeking release from sin's oppression, most of what I heard and read was in abstract terms that were difficult to apply. I'm not trying to put down the people who taught me. I'm only saying that I never found answers that I could clearly understand and apply.

Another obstacle that made it difficult for me to deal with sin was that I never heard whether anyone else struggled with the kinds of sins that were defeating me. One ongoing skirmish I had was with sexual lust. I was extremely shy and insecure around girls, yet I longed for their friendship. Sin always promised to make me feel better about my insecurity, but it left me feeling worse. I assumed that I was the only one who faced struggles like this. After all, I never heard Christian men say it was a problem for them. My conclusion was that this was my unique problem, and I'd better keep my mouth shut or be excommunicated with a swift kick. So I kept my struggles to myself as an act of self-preservation.

The good news is that the Spirit of God honored my hunger for solid biblical principles that I could understand and implement. Over the years, I have searched the Scriptures, studied, meditated on and applied the insights that he gave me. I've kept track of the things God has revealed, picking up helpful insights from a book or remembering the statements in a speaker's sermon that piqued my interest. I've stored those insights away, building my understanding of the nature of sin and our loving Lord's provision for us. Gradually I began to see that the biblical truth, "Sin shall not be master over you," was exactly what our Lord intended (Romans 6:14 NASB). He also created a way for that freedom to be realized. He never mouths idle promises; his promises are anchored in his integrity. Our Lord doesn't lie!

My ministry has put me in touch with Christians young and old from a wide variety of theological backgrounds. I find a consistent theme among them—they cannot articulate a clear biblical strategy for coping with sin in their lives. Many have learned to keep their mouths shut, finding it easier to blunder along with a sin in secret rather than speak openly and be ridiculed. I am positive that some of you who are reading this book are painfully aware of how much sin continues to ravage your life. Some of you have sins that cannot be hidden from the public, and you feel embarrassed about them. Others have habits and addictions that you keep hidden, but they are cancers eating away at your insides. You honestly don't know what to do about these sins because everything you've tried has failed.

Then there are some of you who are highly disciplined and maintain a tight hold on your life. But you know that sin is lurking below the surface like a persistent guerrilla waiting for an opportunity to attack. The truth is that sooner or later it will master you. Your approach is wearing you out and leaving you with little joy. If you lose your grip, you're done. And there are others of you whose sins are less obvious because you are healthy and successful. But a closer scrutiny shows that there are subtle sins thriving in your fields too. After all, "For all have sinned and fall short of the glory of God" (Romans 3:23).

Recently I was invited to be a guest lecturer at a solid, evangelical seminary, and I taught on the problem of sin in the Christian life. Following the class, a graduate student who was auditing the class spoke with me. These are the words I heard: "I've completed three years of seminary education. At no time have I heard a professor address this problem. Yet it's one of the most basic truths I need to grasp." I knew the student well and knew she was going through personal events that left her vulnerable to many of sin's enticing promises. Her statement told me that there are others out there who struggle with this issue and want to hear more about confronting it.

When I set out to discover our Lord's strategy for resolving the problem of sin in our lives, I did so to find the answer for myself. The book you hold in your hand is the fruit of my search, and I want to share what I've learned with you. When I have shared my discoveries with others, they have often asked, "Do you have this in print so that I can read carefully?" or said, "I have a friend that I'd like to share this with." These comments challenged me to write this book. I've endeavored to draw out from the Word of God foundational principles that have helped me understand how sin operates and how God deals with this problem. They are principles that I have tested in my own life with success, and I am confident recommending them to you.

As you read, I encourage you to highlight or underline any insights that challenge your thinking or seem to speak to your heart. Write questions and comments in the margins. Above all, interact with what I've written in a way that helps you think through this issue for yourself.

I get more out of a book when I interact with others as I read it. It is my hope that you will go through this book with your spouse, friend or small group. Others will have insights that you can profit from, and they will profit from yours. I have included a series of questions at the end of each chapter to assist in discussion. If you cannot meet with others, think through them alone.

Many people have their opinions. What we need is clear direction from our Lord's unique revelation, the Bible. When you listen to people talk about the issue of sin, be sure that you separate opinion from biblical truth. Build your foundation on these biblical principles, not on someone's opinions.

Making It Personal

1. Read David's prayer of repentance in Psalm 51. What did David understand about sin?

2. What did David understand about our Lord?

3. What patterns of sin do you observe in your own life?

    a. When are you most prone to sin? (Day of the week, hour of the day, etc.)

    b. In what location are you most prone to sin?

    c. What circumstances precede the times you sin?

    d. Who is present when you sin?

    e. What occurs after you sin?

4. What questions about sin would you like someone to answer in clear, understandable language?

2

DECEIT, DISTORTION & DOOM

*"When we refuse to admit our powerlessness
we are only deceiving ourselves.
The lies we tell ourselves and others are familiar:
'I could stop any time I want to.'
'I'm in control; this one won't hurt anything.'
And all the while, we are inching closer to disaster."*
DAVID STOOP AND STEPHEN ARTERBURN

*"Now the serpent was more crafty than
any of the wild animals the LORD God had made."*
GENESIS 3:1

Two devoted friends wanted to do something special for my wife and me. So they approached us with an enticing question: "If you could go anywhere for a vacation, where would you go?" They offered to let us use their time-share and lent us the directory with a worldwide menu. In no time, Winnie and I were flipping through the pages and eyeing the exotic places that appealed to us.

What if I could offer you an all-expenses-paid vacation to the lushest place on the face of the earth? Where would you choose to go? Imagine that I could fly you to a place of exotic beauty beyond anything you've ever seen before. What if I could send you to the Garden of Eden for a relaxing vacation with Adam and Eve at the time of their innocence? You'd see, hear, taste, smell and feel everything in its pristine beauty and purity. What would you experience? You'd have no reason to fear being robbed, attacked or abused. There would be no traffic snarls. No devastating floods, violent hurricanes or frightening earthquakes. No threatening animals. You could curl up with lions, tigers and cheetahs without fear.

What would it be like to live in an environment totally devoid of sin? No temptation would be eating at you or those around you. What would it be like to enjoy a place that was custom designed by the universe's Master Architect, especially if he could maintain perfect climate control, complete ecological balance and absolute peace among the entire creation? You'd feel the exhilaration of a totally healthy body that surged with energy. And there'd be none of the half-ripened fruit that the supermarkets sell. The most delicious food would be available whenever you felt hungry.

Another bonus would be that every day you would look forward to warm, friendly visits with the Master Designer. All he'd ask is that you honor him and his master plan.

Principle #1: Sin is always rooted in and functions by manipulation, treachery and deceit.

This is the biblical account of Adam and Eve's adventure as recorded in Genesis 1 and 2. It's the utopia we all inwardly long for. But in Genesis 3, a devious adversary ruins everything when he entices Eve to make a fatal decision—one that alters the course of her life and every person born of her lineage. This biblical account is of great significance to us because it reveals truths that are essential to understanding the nature of sin. As we eavesdrop on this profound encounter, we discover the fundamental characteristics of sin as it influences our lives and leads us to dissatisfaction, discouragement, defeat and even destruction.

Fencing with the Devil

The first lesson we learn is that Adam and Eve were not created to cope with the power and subtlety of sin. They did not have the intelligence or discernment to match wits with the evil one as he worked through the serpent. The Garden of Eden was a place of innocence. Eve was naive about the skillful manipulation that the serpent would use against her in their innocent-sounding conversation.

As we read about Eve's encounter with the serpent, we see him planting doubt in her mind and shrewdly leading her into a dangerous whirlpool of sin. He seems so sincere and so caring as he whispers, "You will not surely die. . . . For God knows that when you eat of it your eyes will be opened, and you will be like God, knowing good and evil" (Genesis 3:4-5). Eve is like the proverbial sheep being led to slaughter because she doesn't know that she is a pawn in the serpent's devious plans.

The evil one and his ambassadors can work the same charm on us since we share this same powerlessness over sin. If we deny this, it shows how vulnerable we are. We were born into a world ruled by sin, but we have no natural power to cope with its clever manipulation and deception. I've been told that advertisers use a combination of light-grade motor oil and whipped detergent to show us a glass of beer. When you see a beautiful model with shampoo in her hair, it is probably egg whites or laundry detergent whipped into a creamy foam. And that appetizing rice you saw on the TV commercial was actually small pebbles that were used because they don't stick together like rice does. We naively thought it was the real thing and were tricked into thinking it was what we wanted. Perhaps we should be less quick to judge Eve.

When I understood sin's power, I was freed from a trap that had kept me in bondage. For years, pastors and Bible teachers taught me that God was holding me accountable to lick the sin problem in my life. I assumed that I was responsible to cope with sin with my own strength, to muster up an inner reserve of personal power and put down incessant hungers that wouldn't leave me alone. I thought that my heavenly Father was saying to me, "I expect you to strain every muscle to resist sin's temptation. Memorize the Bible. Learn to fend off Satan's attacks like a fencer parries his opponent. Then when you have given it your best shot, call on me, and I'll rush in and rescue you." In truth, whenever I tried to fence with the devil, I got so engrossed in the problem that I'd forget to call on the Lord until I was already defeated.

Then one day our Lord's truth penetrated my mind, and it hit me like a ton of bricks. *My Lord never intended me to cope with sin on my own.* He didn't create me with that ability. I wasn't designed to fence with the devil. I cannot describe how relieved I felt. A huge load rolled off my back. The years of guilt and shame I felt for not being strong enough to ward off the evil one left me. Finally I could see that someone mightier than I had to face the evil enemy. What a relief to know that the years of futile striving had ended!

I live in Phoenix, Arizona, where backyard swimming pools dot the landscape. Almost every day during the summer months, the local newscasters warn parents about the dangers of children falling into pools and drowning. Yet drownings continue to occur frequently because parents fail to realize how quickly children can be seduced by water and how defenseless they are in it. Children have a beautiful innocence, but it's an innocence that must be guarded by someone older, wiser and stronger. In the same manner, we face forces beyond our ability. Until we fully acknowledge our absolute dependence on our wise, all-powerful Father, we will not find his answer to the problem of sin in our lives.

Oswald Chambers has stated it clearly and powerfully: "Purity in God's children is not the outcome of obedience to His law, but the result of the supernatural work of His grace. 'I will cleanse you'; 'I will give you a new heart'; 'I will put my Spirit within you and cause you to walk in My statutes'; 'I will do it all.'"[1]

When we look at the great Old Testament "heroes," we are struck by their inability to cope with the problem of sin in their lives. Abraham practiced deceit—and passed it on to his son Isaac (Genesis 12:10-20). Sarah held bitterness toward Hagar, her servant, when Hagar had a child by Abraham, even though Sarah foolishly initiated the plan (Genesis 16:1-5). Jacob had a lifelong history of deceit and manipulation against his father, brother and father-in-law. And when we review King David's record, we see that he repeatedly succumbed to sin's temptation. My intent is not to malign these individuals but to stress that they are clear examples that we were not created to cope with sin. We have to have an outside source of protection and strength. The answer is not to try harder.

As I ponder this issue, I am reminded of an incident I observed several years ago. I was sitting in the kitchen of a mobile home in a rural community north of Phoenix, Arizona. Suddenly I heard a thump and realized that a zealous bird had flown beak first into the kitchen window. About a minute later, I heard the thump again and saw the bird fly back to the branch. It happened over and over again. My first reaction was, "That is one crazy bird!" But then I realized that this confused creature was seeing his reflection in the windowpane and thought he was seeing a new friend to play with or a rival threatening his territory. However, because he wasn't created with the ability to realize his deception, he continued to fly into the window. How like the bird we are! Too often we are powerless to recognize an illusion and are repeatedly drawn to it, only to be knocked for a loop again and again.

Created to Be Led

I discovered a second life principle as I studied Adam and Eve's account in the Garden. I realized that *we were created to be led.* We were created to submit to another who is wiser, stronger and holds all things together. He is the ultimate Sovereign, the absolute Ruler, and the One with maximum power. He alone can protect us from evil. He alone can rule over evil powers.

The serpent enticed Eve to step outside her circle of loving protection, where she was dependant on God, and become an independent, vulnerable person. Here is what I hear in the evil one's manipulative message: "Your God is limiting you and doing it for his own advantage. He doesn't want you to reach your full potential. You can be like God, but you'll never achieve it if you keep yourself under his thumb. Step out and be your own person." Eve believed what she heard and took that fatal step outside her Lord's leadership. And she immediately became vulnerable to anything and anybody.

Jesus said, "When you bow down before the Lord and admit your dependence on him, he will lift you up and give you honor" (Matthew 11:28-30 NLT). James said, "Humble yourselves before the Lord, and he will lift you up" (James 4:10). Both remind us that we were created to live a dependent relationship with our Sovereign, and only when we step joyfully into his leadership will we be safe from sin's persistent assault. In a society that shouts, "Do your own thing. Be your own person," the message of Scripture sounds confining and out of place. But God never lies to us. His Word is always true; his Word alone can lead us to freedom.

The person who falls for the lie that he or she can be a self-made, self-sufficient individual has fallen for one of the biggest lies around. It may sound rude to say, but that person is a fool.

While talking with my friend Gerald about this issue, he made the following comment: "I think I have been led by those who I have let influence me. I can think of specific things I do that I have picked up from others." Then he made the observation that one of the reasons our Lord calls us sheep is that sheep have to be led (Psalm 23; John 10:1-21). We know that others influence our decisions and actions; what we need to grasp is how crucial it is that our Lord be the ultimate leader of our lives.

As I pondered this truth, I thought of two questions that we all have to answer. The first is, "Am I *willing* to be led?" I find an urge within my natural humanity—apart from Christ—to be free from any restraints. There are many things that I want to do, and I don't want anyone to limit my opportunities or suppress my longings. In some ways it's similar to the Christian woman who tells her friend, "I know I shouldn't, but I want to have an affair." Somehow she has allowed herself to listen to the subtle voice that promised that an affair would be pleasurable and fulfilling and would lead to a better life.

After I'd asked the first question about my willingness, I found a second question: "Do I *desire* the Lord to be ruler of my life?" I believe that our Lord is calling us to a lifestyle in which we yearn to be led, we hunger for unity with our Lord, and we pursue his counsel. We've recognized our natural tendency to want independence, but we also hear our spirit crying out, "My Lord, I want to live under the shadow of your presence. Not my will but yours be done. Lead me!"

Beauty and the Beast

Wisteria is a plant that attracts people with its beautiful flowers and fragrant aroma. It grows so heartily that we're tempted to say, "I'd love to have some of that growing in my backyard." But once this alluring plant gets established, it begins to assert its muscle and dominate everything it touches. An article in *Southern Living* described it this way:

> Wisteria grows and grows and grows some more. Its slender, twining tendrils eventually become thick, muscular limbs that wrap around trees, fences, and arbors like the coils of a python. Wisteria makes shredded wheat out of lattice and bends iron railings like taffy. And if it escapes to the woods, look out.[2]

When wisteria attaches itself to something, it tries to twist it into a form that will serve the plant's purpose. Its beauty attracts us, and we bring it in and plant it in our garden. But the plant then demonstrates a power over our environment that we didn't realize it had. In a similar manner, when sin makes its appeal to us, it always looks, feels, tastes and sounds attractive. If you carefully observe the serpent's interaction with Eve, you'll discover the basic distortions that sin creates. It wraps itself around our thought patterns and twists them so we don't see things as they really are. We begin to see what the power of sin wants us to see.

Sin effectively distorts our view of our Lord. Notice that the serpent's basic tactic is to discredit Eve's God. He challenges her to reexamine who her God really is. He implies that her

Sovereign's motives are selfish. He says, "God doesn't want you to be like him." He implies that God is trying to limit her and keep her from achieving her full potential. He tells her, "You'll be like God." This is an important principle to remember: Satan's first and foremost attack will be upon God's motives and character. How many Christians do you know who are angry with our Lord because they interpreted life circumstances as God's indifference or punishment? I wonder where that idea came from!

The evil one's strategy is always to distort and discredit our Lord. He tries to convince us that our Lord is

• not reliable. He won't be there when we need him.
• not generous. He won't supply our needs.
• not loving. We're not perfect enough, not important enough, etc.
• not satisfying. He is boring, unfulfilling, cold, impersonal and so on.
• not caring. He has more important things to do. We're not worthy of his care.
• not available when we need him. We can't count on him.

If he can sow these seeds of doubt in our minds, he can drive a wedge into our relationship with our Father and pull us under his control. But remember that if we are pestered with doubts similar to the ones suggested above, they tell us more about ourselves than our Lord. He has clearly told us who he is and has demonstrated his commitment from generation to generation. We've listened to the deceiver. We got sucked in and began to question our loving Lord's integrity and commitment to us. We'd do well to heed Jesus' counsel in Mark 4:24 and be careful of what we listen to.

I found David Roper's insight on this helpful. He says, "It occurred to me one day that everything the devil does is designed for one purpose only: to draw us away from God's love. He does so not because he hates us, but because he hates God and will do anything to break His heart, and nothing breaks God's heart more than being separated from those He loves."[3]

I find it fascinating that the biblical account gives no indication that either Adam or Eve went back to their Creator for his perspective after Eve listened to the serpent's tirade against him. I wonder why she didn't share her confusion, doubts and questions with him? Why didn't she give him an opportunity to clarify the matter? But lest we judge Eve too severely, we need to remember that we too are more prone to listen to the enemy than to trust our Father who has pledged his loyalty and love to us.

Sin distorts our view of ourselves. Adam and Eve were created to be dependent upon a wise, loving and protective Sovereign. Apart from him they were weak, vulnerable and helpless. But the serpent convinced Eve that she could take matters into her own hands and create a more fulfilling future for herself apart from her sovereign Lord. She discovered too late that she'd been duped and would suffer the consequences for the rest of her life.

The nature of my ministry has brought me in contact with hundreds of individuals who share their life issues with me. It's obvious to me that early in life we are subject to innumerable voices that endeavor to tell us who we are, what we should do, what we can become and what the good life is. There has never been a day like the present one in which we are barraged with messages from the time we wake until the time we go to sleep. Everywhere we turn, we are told what to think, what to buy, what to wear, how to look and how to relate to others. For most of us, only a tiny percentage of these voices reflect our Lord's point of view. It is difficult not to get the world's distorted view of who we are, whom we can trust, what is real and what is important. That's why the apostle Paul warned us against letting the world's system squeeze us into its mold (Romans 12:1-2).

What makes this difficult is that these voices do not merely appeal to our intellect. What gives them great power is that they appeal to our emotions. They capture our feelings and feed on our longings and desires. Sometimes they inflame valid desires, but in the wrong direction. At other times the voices tempt us to seek satisfaction for desires that are not necessary for a joyful life. But we continue to let our mind and emotions feed on the desires until they gain great power over us. Then we take the first step . . . and the second step . . . until they are controlling our lives.

Sin always looks like an attractive alternative. The evil one made sin look attractive to Eve. Sin sounded so logical and sensible. It looked like a chance to expand herself and to experience a more fulfilling life. The serpent said to Eve, "You can be God." Imagine her saying to herself, "Wow! This is wonderful. I'm thankful for this kind, insightful serpent that is so loving as to show me this opportunity. Only good can come from this." In a clever sleight of hand, Satan makes evil look very good. It always looks and feels like something better than what we're experiencing. Only after the event do we realize that it leads to heartache, defeat and destruction. When sin is making its appeal, we think, "I don't want to miss out on this," but after we've acted on it we think, "What a fool I was. I can't believe that I fell for it."

I heard a gripping analogy of sin that is a good reminder of sin's subtle danger. I've been told that Eskimo hunters have an ingenious method for killing wolves. First the hunter hones his knife to a razor-sharp edge. Then he coats the blade in blood and lets it freeze. He continues adding layer upon layer of blood until he has a frozen blood popsicle. Finally he fixes the knife in the frozen ground with the blade pointed up.

Later a hungry wolf catches the scent of blood, and his nose leads him to what he thinks will be a great feast. With great zest he begins to lick the blood from the knife. As the taste of blood heightens his appetite, his craving becomes inflamed, and he licks more feverishly. He doesn't realize the moment when his tongue reaches the naked blade and is sliced by the razor-sharp edge. Unknown to him, he is now being satisfied by his own warm blood. When the Eskimo hunter returns the next morning, he finds a dead wolf.

I don't mean to offend with my illustration, but I use it to help us realize that the appeal of sin is no less deadly. When we become addicted to its power, something within us is dying. A crafty enemy who has no mercy on us plants his subtle scent. The true nature of sin is hidden under an attractive coat of pleasures. Then our emotions kick in, and we never realize when our tongue has touched the knife. Too late we realize that we yielded to a false promise and must pay the consequence of our folly.

Sin distorts our true needs and our Lord's means to meet them. In a later chapter we'll look at the importance of valid needs in our life. At this point I want you to understand that sin exploits us by offering an appealing substitute to meet a valid need. Sin bypasses God's intended solution for our needs and causes us to try to meet the needs with appealing, invalid solutions. For example, all of us have been created for intimate relationships. Our Lord has established healthy, fulfilling ways for intimacy to occur with his full blessing. But the crafty one distorts our thinking about God's ways and convinces us that intimacy can be achieved more easily, more quickly or with more pleasure outside of God's ways. It's not difficult to think of examples of this from our own lives, our own families and our own friends.

So what have we learned about the problem of sin? Sin is always rooted in and functions by manipulation, treachery and deceit. And we're not smart enough or strong enough by ourselves to stand against it. When Adam and Eve short-circuited their intimate relationship with their Lord, they became open to manipulation and deceit. Their view of reality was distorted when they became convinced to follow their own path, and consequently their Eden life was destroyed. Instead of embracing God's love, they now hid from him in fear. Sin changed their perception of this wise, loving and faithful Person.

"The man and his wife heard the sound of the LORD God as he was walking in the garden in the cool of the day, and they hid from the LORD God among the trees of the garden" (Genesis 3:8). Instead of openness and transparency, Adam and Eve now experienced shame, with no adequate way to remove it. "Then the eyes of both of them were opened, and they realized they were naked; so they sewed fig leaves together and made coverings for themselves" (Genesis 3:7). Instead of being in loving relationships, they began to blame their disobedience on others. "The woman said, 'The serpent deceived me, and I ate'" (Genesis 3:12).

How about you? What do you need to learn from this episode in Adam and Eve's life? Do you daily embrace the principles I've outlined in this chapter? Are they so rooted in your thinking that you operate from that point of view?

Making It Personal

1. In what ways has sin deceived you?

2. What is the biblical approach to dealing with the devil? Is this clear in your mind?

3. What happens when a person tries to deal with sin in his or her own strength? What is your method of dealing with the sin in your life?

4. What is your honest answer to these two questions: (a) Am I *willing* to have my Lord be the leader of my life? And (b) Do I *desire* the Lord to be the leader of my life?

5. How do you think sin has distorted the way you view our Lord?

6. Earlier I listed many distortions we can have about our Lord. Take the list below and find statements in the Bible that refute these deceptions:

• The Lord is not reliable. He won't be there when we need him.

• The Lord is not generous. He won't supply our needs.

• The Lord is not loving. We're not perfect enough, not important enough and so on.

• The Lord is not satisfying. He is boring, unfulfilling, cold, impersonal and so on.

• The Lord is not caring. He has more important things to do. We're not worthy of his care.

• The Lord is not available when we need him. We can't count on him.

7. How has sin distorted the way you think and feel about yourself?

8. How has sin attached itself to valid needs in your life? What have been the consequences?

3

THE ORIGINAL
GENE THERAPY

"My sin, O, the bliss of this glorious thought,
My sin not in part but the whole,
Is nailed to the cross and I bear it no more,
Praise the Lord, praise the Lord, O my soul."
HORATIO G. SPAFFORD

"For just as through the disobedience of the one man the
many were made sinners, so also through the obedience
of the one man the many will be made righteous."
ROMANS 5:19

Pham Quoc Phong was born in Vung Tau City, Vietnam, on July 29, 1999, to a single mother living in poverty. With no hope of meeting her son's basic needs, this loving mother placed him up for adoption. As this scenario unfolded, a young couple half a world away, in Phoenix, Arizona, was praying about adopting a foreign-born child to complement their pre-school-age son and daughter. Thus, on December 2, 1999, Matthew and Jill Bachali flew to Vietnam to welcome young Phong into their family.

Part of the adoption procedure involved meeting Phong's birth mother. As they sat at a table, Jill got the impression that Phong's mother was a humble, shy woman who loved her son very much. But because she was so poverty-stricken she had no means to care for him. She wept and said she would miss Phong very much. Her words through the interpreter were, "Take care of my baby."

Through the interpreter, Matthew asked Phong's mother if there was anything that she would like her son to know about his birth family. She replied, "I'd like him to know that he has a brother." As Matthew sought to clarify this fact, he and Jill were stunned to discover that Phong had a *twin* brother, Pham Quoc Phu, who had been assigned to a French adoption agency. Further investigation revealed that Phu's adoption had fallen through and there was the possibility that Matthew and Jill could adopt him also. This would require filing new adoption papers and returning to Vietnam several months later. The emotionally drained couple boarded the jetliner with their new son to return to Phoenix and begin the adoption process over again.

Matthew and Jill changed Phong's name to Henry Cooper Bachali. Through the grace of God, Henry left behind a land of political oppression to become a citizen of the United States. Instead of poverty he will know abundance and will have the opportunity to receive a good education. He has a loving, devoted father and mother. He is learning a new language, getting to know his new siblings and making new friends. Henry is being reared in a home devoted to honoring Jesus Christ rather than Buddha.

Phong was dramatically severed from his old family tree in which he would have had no real future. Though his birth mother loved him, she had no relationship with our Lord and was trapped in poverty, living under an oppressive government. Now her child is grafted into a new family tree and will have the opportunity to grow into a healthy young man—

physically, mentally, emotionally, socially and spiritually. Knowing Jill and Matthew, I'm certain that Henry will receive an abundance of smiles, hugs and kisses. He will be prayed for, nurtured, taught and encouraged by loving Christian adoptive parents who are happy to have him in their lives. Matthew and Jill see him as a gift from our Lord.

The Divine Grafting

The incident I've described to you illustrates an even greater adoption that has profound implications for those who experience it firsthand. In Romans 6, the apostle Paul reminds his readers of an adoption that was completed with Jesus' death and involves most of us reading this book. As he explores the problem of sin, he describes a far-reaching truth. Consider his words:

> If we've left the country where sin is sovereign, how can we still live in our old house there? Or didn't you realize we packed up and left there for good? That is what happened in baptism. When we went under the water, we left the old country of sin behind; when we came up out of the water, we entered into the new country of grace—a new life in a new land!
>
> That's what baptism into the life of Jesus means. When we are lowered into the water, it is like the burial of Jesus; when we are raised up out of the water, it is like the resurrection of Jesus. Each of us is raised into a light-filled world by our Father so that we can see where we're going in our new grace-sovereign country. (Romans 6:2-4 The Message)

Spiritually we were all like Phong before he became Henry Cooper Bachali. The Bible states clearly that all of us were born into the family line of our forefather, Adam. Paul says, "Therefore, just as sin came into the world through one man, and death came through sin, and so death spread to all because all have sinned" (Romans 5:12 NRSV). Through Adam's family tree we were infected with a sin "gene." (I'm using the word *gene* symbolically.) Sin and death have a hereditary origin dating back to Adam. The problem you and I face is not that we commit innumerable acts of sin. It's a much deeper dilemma. We enter this world with a deeply rooted predisposition toward sin. Perhaps you've heard this succinct truism: "I'm not a sinner because I sin, but I sin because I'm a sinner." That's the solemn news: Something is fundamentally wrong within us that conditions us to sin.

Principle #2: *Sin is a hereditary disease of the flesh.*

In the previous chapter, I reminded you that we were not created to cope with sin. Adam and Eve had no internal defense mechanism to protect them against the enemy. Their defense was external. Their sovereign God could protect them against anything and anybody as long as they remained loyal to his leadership. As long as they let him be their refuge and strength, they were perfectly safe. But when they stepped outside the sphere of his protection, they were completely vulnerable. When they succumbed to the serpent's influence and sin penetrated their lives, they acquired a second weakness—they were infected with a genetic disease that would curse everyone born of their seed.

Our problem is not that we sin; our problem is that we are spiritually diseased. The acts of sin merely tell us that something is malfunctioning inside. They are a symptom of a deeper problem. We are condemned with an incurable plague that corrodes our soul, leaving us powerless to do what we ought to do and causing us to give in to what we want to do. There is no cure that is effective for this damning affliction. No vitamins, herbs or medicine can cure this ailment. We have no strength or ability within ourselves to fight it. Apart from a supernatural power, we are doomed. It's that serious.

Amazing Grace! How Sweet the Sound!

Let's return for a second look at Phong before he became Henry. He is a picture of our condition. He was thrust into a world that condemned him to poverty, tyranny and hopelessness. All of his proud Vietnamese heritage and all of his birth mother's tender love could not deliver him. And he was powerless to help himself. I'm reminded of Paul's words, "When we were still powerless, Christ died for the ungodly" (Romans 5:6). The odds are overwhelming that Phong would have been trapped into the same life as his mother had he not been rescued by adoption. By pure grace, a couple came along and welcomed him into their family. They asked nothing of him; they gave him the unsolicited, unearned and undeserved gift of a new life. He was grafted into the Bachali family tree and will bear the fruit of the new union.

The Word of God makes clear the seriousness of our sin problem. We are told that we were born into Adam's lineage, which condemns us with Adam's disease. Every person born of Adam is born with the genetic nature to sin. Paul says, "We have already made the charge that Jews and Gentiles alike are all under sin" (Romans 3:9), and later, "For all have sinned and fall short of the glory of God" (Romans 3:23).

Thank God we are not left to despair in this hopeless situation. Jesus Christ bore the penalty for our sins with his death on the cross and radically changed our condition. We discover that "just as through the disobedience of the one man [Adam] the many were made sinners, so also through the obedience of the one man [Jesus Christ] the many will be made righteous" (Romans 5:19). And in Romans 6:3-5 we are told that those who trust in the death of Christ on their behalf are grafted into Christ himself. Being born again severs us from Adam's family tree and grafts us into Christ's family tree. Ray Stedman writes, "All that we were as a natural-born human being ended when we believed in Jesus."[1]

The death of Christ on our behalf is not just a theological fact; it has far-reaching implications. For one thing, it means that when I am grafted, or adopted, into Jesus Christ, the curse that I receive in Adam is canceled out. I am no longer in Adam's lineage. My life is inseparably linked to Jesus Christ. You might say that the *real* me—the born again me—has Christ's genes.

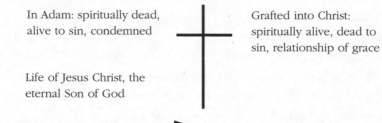

In Adam: spiritually dead, alive to sin, condemned

Grafted into Christ: spiritually alive, dead to sin, relationship of grace

Life of Jesus Christ, the eternal Son of God

Figure 1

Figure 1 visually illustrates the transaction that occurs in the lives of all who trust in the work of Jesus Christ. In some manner beyond full comprehension, we have been adopted into our heavenly Father's family with all rights, privileges and benefits. He treats us as he treats Christ because we are grafted into his beloved Son. The Bible says that we were "dead in [our] transgressions and sins, in which [we] used to live" (Ephesians 2:1). Now we are "made alive with Christ" and raised up "with Christ and seated . . . with him in the heavenly realms in Christ Jesus" (Ephesians 2:5-6).

We need to return again to Henry Cooper Bachali. When he was adopted into Matthew and Jill's family, his connection to his birth mother and father ended. They no longer have rights to or authority over Henry. We might say that he died to their authority. He has died to the authority of the country in which he was born. He is now alive to new loving parents and to a nation of freedom and opportunity. He has a new name, a new citizenship, a new language, a new home and new siblings. He died to the old and is alive to the new. He will grow up aware of his original lineage, but he will live free from its dominion. In a real sense, he is a new creature created in the Bachali family.

As I pondered this modern-day parable, I thought about what would happen if Henry wanted to visit Vietnam as an adult. He would not know the language, he would have to apply for a visa because he is no longer a citizen. In a similar way, we were "rescued . . . from the dominion of darkness and brought . . . into the kingdom of the Son he loves, in whom we have redemption, the forgiveness of sins" (Colossians 1:13-14). Our Lord's work of redemption on our behalf has *literally* taken us from the authority and dominion of sin and brought us into the closest, most intimate relationship possible with Jesus Christ. Jesus has restored what Adam and Eve lost for us. In the same way that Henry's birth mother and the country of Vietnam have no authority over him, sin has no authority to rule over you. Until you grasp this essential truth, sin will continue to hold unauthorized power over you. You have been freed, but you must claim that freedom with firm conviction.

This has great implications for our lives. Before we were born again, we were at the mercy of sin. We were in Adam's lineage and enslaved to sin. It held us with an iron fist until our Lord's sovereign grace dethroned it. Now we live in a new land. We have a new citizenship. We have a new spiritual life. We have a new Sovereign to whom we bow and give allegiance and to whom false powers will release control. But we will find no lasting relief from the problem of sin until we understand that we have a new lineage.

I took a new step forward when I decided to trust that what the Word of God said about these issues was true. When I said, "Yes, it's true," I was faced with a second step—to make that truth the basis of my actions and decisions. This act of trust and obedience is most noticeable in moments of crisis. That's when I can tell whether I am relying on my own strategies or on Scripture. While our Lord is the authoritative Power acting on my behalf, I participate in it by embracing what he has said and refusing to depart from it.

Freedom from Sin's Dominion

The powers of sin and darkness have no authority over you as a child living under the protection of a powerful God. The tragedy is that many of us do not grasp this liberating truth but continue to live under the dominion of a power that has been nullified.

Prior to the Civil War, slaves were the property of their masters. But on September 22, 1862, President Abraham Lincoln signed the Emancipation Proclamation that would take effect on January 1 of the following year. The proclamation stated:

> That on the first day of January, in the year of our Lord one thousand eight hundred and sixty-three, all persons held as slaves within any State or designated part of a State, the people whereof shall then be in rebellion against the United States, shall be then, thenceforward and forever free, and the Executive Government of the United States, including the military and

naval authority thereof, will recognize and maintain the freedom of such persons, and will do no act or acts to repress such persons, or any of them, in any efforts they may make for their actual freedom.

Every slave was granted freedom from oppression and the proclamation was enforced by any means the government saw fit to use. The masters no longer had authority over their slaves. Every slave had legal freedom to move about as he or she pleased. But unfortunately two situations caused many liberated slaves to continue to live in bondage. First, some former slaves lived on remote farms and never heard the good news that freedom had been granted. They continued in bondage even though they were free. Second, some masters threatened and intimidated their slaves into believing that they must continue living under the master's tyrannical control. In both cases, although freedom was theirs, false masters would dominate them.

Think about these questions:

• Have you heard, and do you believe, the good news that sin has no authority over you?

• Are you allowing sin to intimidate you by claiming an illegitimate authority?

• Is an unauthorized power ruling your life?

The Word of God teaches us that if we confess Jesus Christ as our sin-bearer we are delivered from the kingdom of darkness—the kingdom of being in slavery to sin—and transferred into the kingdom of light—the kingdom of serving an almighty, loving God. Until we believe this truth and act on it, we will be pushed around, manipulated and enslaved to a false authority.

This change of citizenship radically changes our relationship to sin. The apostle Paul said it clearly in Romans:

- "We died to sin; how can we live in it any longer?" (Romans 6:2).
- "Count yourselves dead to sin but alive to God in Christ Jesus" (Romans 6:11).
- "Sin shall not be your master, because you are not under law, but under grace" (Romans 6:14).

Sometimes it's hard for us to imagine what it means that sin shall no longer be our master. This next example may help. In 1838 slavery was abolished in Jamaica. The law was to take effect on August 1 of that year. A crowd of freed slaves met at the beach the night before the law took effect to celebrate their new freedom. The mood was festive yet solemn. Someone arrived with a large mahogany casket and placed it on the sandy beach next to a hole that had been dug. As the former slaves arrived, they tossed items into the coffin that represented their oppressed lives: leg-irons, whips, chains, locks, etc.

Then just before the midnight hour struck, the casket was lowered into the pit. As the celebrants filled the hole, they began singing, "Praise God from whom all blessings flow, praise him all creatures here below." This powerful event etched on the participants' minds the reality that they were free from the demeaning oppression. Perhaps we too, as individuals released from the slavery to sin, need to hold a funeral to confirm this reality.

The Rest of the Story

Perhaps you're wondering what happened to Henry's twin brother, Phu. Matthew and Jill traveled to Vietnam a second time to meet with Henry's mother. Jill observed that she was restless, nervous and agitated. Henry's mother said that Phu was at her sister's house and they needed to go there. "My sister owns me," she said. When they arrived, the sister took over the conversation. She was brusque and businesslike. She began to bargain for the life of her nephew, demanding $3000, a new house for Henry's mother and ongoing support. She wanted to find relief from poverty by illegally selling Henry's twin brother. With tears streaming down his face, Matthew had to tell her, "I can't do that."

With broken hearts, they returned to the United States without Henry's brother. When the Bachalis told me about this incident, I was struck with its implications. Here were two identical brothers of the same parents, but with radically different futures. Henry will grow up in the realm of God's love, grace and truth. But because his brother could not be taken from oppression and poverty, he will most likely grow up in darkness.

I expect that you still have many questions about the way sin exploits the child of God, but before we get to that, you should apply the two truths I've demonstrated in this chapter. First, we were born in sin. It is an active force that produces sinful behavior. Second, through the work of Jesus Christ we exchanged our family lineage, and sin's power to rule over us was broken. We were taken out of Adam's family tree and placed into Christ's family tree. That transaction removed sin's authority over you as a child of God. You owe no allegiance to sin. It has no rightful basis to harass or intimidate you. You must possess a settled conviction as you stand up to this enemy and make clear that you know your spiritual citizenship and your new master. Loyalty and submission to your new ruler is crucial.

I've read that skulls from ancient Indians are on display in a Chicago museum. The skulls have holes bored in them because the Indians believed the holes would let the demons out. Today we hear many confusing and bizarre ideas for ridding our lives of sinful behaviors and habits. We don't need to bore holes in our skulls. We don't need to lash ourselves with whips to beat sin out. Our Lord has a better way. We merely need to apply what is so clearly taught in the Word of God.

Our mighty Lord has not left you defenseless against the power of sin in your flesh. But if you don't know that he has made a provision and don't understand how to apply it to the problem, you'll be no better off. You must develop a settled conviction about this biblical truth and then act on it with decisiveness at the moment of temptation (1 Corinthians 10:13). It's a first step in moving from sin's control to our Lord's deliverance.

Making It Personal

1. How have you felt intimidated or manipulated by internal pressure to sin?

2. In words that are clear to you, summarize the principles this chapter teaches. Identify Scriptures that support each principle. You may want to begin with Romans 6.

3. When you find yourself under sin's attack or appeal, what biblical resources do you turn to?

4. Do you need to hold a funeral, as the Jamaicans did, to celebrate your deliverance from slavery?

5. Read Psalm 51. After being discovered in his sin with Bathsheba, David prays this prayer. Note the verbs in the psalm. You might find it helpful to rewrite the psalm, making it your own personal prayer with your own words. (For example, "Only God can blot out my transgression.") One of my friends did this and said that it helped him realize that Christ was sufficient to deal with his sins.

4

MY SIN—HIS GRACE

*"The Word 'grace' is unquestionably the most
significant single word in the Bible."*
ILION T. JONES

*"But where sin increased,
grace increased all the more."*
ROMANS 5:20

As the years have passed, I've found myself consistently drawn to Jesus' parable of the prodigal son in Luke 15. It has been like a never-failing magnet that keeps drawing me back to absorb a remarkable truth. It took me some time to grasp what it was that I found so appealing in the account. I asked myself, "Why does it speak so powerfully to me? What void does it fill?"

As I digested the truth embodied in the parable, a gentle hush began to penetrate my spirit. I could now see that what has drawn me back to this story is the love the father lavishes on his dirty, defeated and disgraceful son. Yes, it takes my breath away to realize that there is someone whose love is so rich, so deep and so pure. Jesus stands before us as one who is so extravagant in his love that we stand spellbound. Then I realized that it was this same power that drew society's out-casts—those who knew the pain, discouragement and empti-ness of sin—into a relationship with our Lord Jesus. He spoke words and exhibited attitudes that refreshed them and filled them with hope. And, ironically, it was this same power that so violently offended the religious elite. The father's response to his son's return is out of character with how parents would typically treat a child who had abused, scorned and rejected them.

I hungered for that kind of love for so many years. Then I discovered it in my Lord.

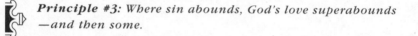

Principle #3: *Where sin abounds, God's love superabounds —and then some.*

Most of us find it mind-boggling that there is a love that pen-etrates so deeply into our failures, our violations and our sins, like an ointment going deep to soothe aching muscles. We find it hard to comprehend that someone loves us so completely that our sin can never diminish the power of his love. It causes us to bow our head in genuine humility, knowing that we are continually loved despite our sin. We might even find our-selves weeping with gratitude because the beloved Lover came into our lives.

I do.

I keep going back to Jesus' parable because it touches my hunger for intimacy with my Lord and reminds me of the lov-ing quality of God's character. I need to feel my Father's arms around me, embracing me with passionate love. The parable reminds me that he can fulfill that need. By faith I gaze into his eyes and see that instead of bitterness, resentment or hostility there is high-octane love. I see that he's excited that I'm home again even though my dirty clothes remind me that I don't deserve such unconditional love. When I consider the privilege of being loved in such an extravagant, undeserving way, gratitude wells up in my heart and spills over the rim. It prompts me to bow my head in heartfelt worship to this glorious Sovereign.

An Amazing Bible Truth

Paul explores this intriguing theme in Romans 5. He reminds us that sin was introduced to the human race through Adam. Ever since Adam, all of sin's destructive power has been unleashed against us to "boss us around." But now through the love of our blessed Father and through Jesus Christ's willingness to take our penalty upon himself, we have been invited into our Father's family with all the rights and privileges family members enjoy. In Romans 5:12-21, Paul contrasts what sin accomplished through Adam to what God's grace accomplished through Christ. As he develops this comparison, he makes a profound statement. Writing under the inspiration of the Spirit, Paul says, "Where sin increased, grace increased all the more" (Romans 5:20). A literal translation is "Where sin increased, grace superabounded with more added to that."[1] If sin leaps the high hurdles, God's grace leaps the highest skyscraper. If sin can swim Lake Erie, God's grace can swim the Atlantic Ocean without getting tired. The power of sin can never match our Lord's gracious love.

I had read and reread this verse for years. Then one day the underlying truth hit me like a sledgehammer. I felt a sense of excitement as I realized the implications of what Paul was saying. For the first time, I grasped the fact that for the child of God, there is always a love that superabounds beyond his or her sin. Somebody loves me despite my sin. Somebody loves me before I sin. Somebody loves me when I'm sinning. And somebody loves me after I've sinned. My Lord's love for me always super-abounds beyond my sin. Ray Stedman says, "All my life, as many times as I sin, I cannot out-sin the grace of God. No matter how many trespasses are involved in my record, there is freedom in Christ and forgiveness for all of them."[2]

I wonder if this might describe your experience. You sin, know you're guilty and feel ashamed about what you've done. In your mind you think something like, "Boy, God is mad at me now. He must be really ticked off, and he won't want to have anything to do with me. I know I'll get the cold shoulder. He's probably devising some plan to make me pay for what I've done." Even though you pray and admit your sin and promise to try harder the next time, you still have that uncomfortable feeling that he's upset with you and wants to get even.

Hold on to that thought for a minute while we return to the father of the prodigal son. Doesn't it amaze you that when he sees his son, his thoughts are not on the son's sin but on how much he loves him and has missed his presence at the family table? There is absolutely no evidence that he is thinking about getting revenge for what his son has done to him. Every action is an act of love not anger or revenge. Every action toward his foolish, wayward son communicates the tender passion that rises up in the father's breast. He exhibits the love in such lavish ways that we are left with our mouths open in amazement. Even though the son has committed evil actions toward his father, the father is eager for restoration not revenge.

If you are impressed with this picture Jesus paints for us, remember that our heavenly Father lavished compassion and kindness on you and me when he sent his beloved Son to the cross. The lavishness of Jesus' love is undeniable as we see him hanging on that cruel cross, bearing our sins and taking our penalty upon himself. What an outpouring! What an eternal statement of his lavish love. This only makes sense when we understand that our Lord's love is based on who *he* is and not on who *we* are. He doesn't look inside us to see if there is something that makes us worthy to be loved. Rather he has "poured out his love into our hearts by the Holy Spirit" because that's his nature, not because we deserve it (Romans 5:5).

Our Lord's Baffling Strategy

I vividly remember when I was in my mid-twenties and experienced something that left me baffled. I'd sin and feel shamed. In my mind I'd be thinking, "Norm, you're going to get it now. The Lord is fed up with you and is about to unleash his indignation on you." But then something would happen that confused me. He'd bless me instead! That really confused me. I was forced to conclude that he was showing me that his love was not based on my being good or bad. It was as though he was saying, "I'm not going to let you think that you have to earn my love. It is given as a free gift." Believe me, it got my attention.

Do you recognize that our Lord's ways are radically different from ours? We try to shape people's behavior by holding conditional love like a carrot in front of them. It catches us off guard when God deals with our sin problem by putting something infinitely greater in its place. He makes sin look cheap, empty and pointless by putting something before us that is abundant, touching and satisfying. We keep expecting to be punished for our sin, but because Jesus Christ took our punishment, God is free to lavish his love on us.

Lest you think that such love will make us careless in our conduct or more prone to sin, I'll guarantee you it doesn't work that way. This kind of love brings us to our knees in humility and worship. Words cannot express the emotions of one who receives such undeserved love, and I speak from experience. The result is profound gratitude that deepens our longing to live godly lives that honor our beloved Father.

It is clear that until we know a love that is greater than our sin, we will never be freed from sin's domination. For years I had it backwards. I thought I had to prove my love to God with the purity of my life. Instead I found that it was his love that brought purity, not mine. Until we know that he is more concerned with us than with our sin, we will not find freedom. This works on two levels. On one level, it works in our relationship with our Lord. Until we rest in his love that transcends our sin, we will never find the power to cope adequately with the power of sin. On the second level, this principle works in our relationships with fellow Christians. Until we know that we are loved despite our sin, we'll return to our sin to fill our emptiness. Yes, that's right—until we know a love that fills our need for love, we'll return to our sin to fill it.

Our Lord often demonstrates his amazing love for us through the life of another Christian. I was trapped in habits of sin for years because I believed I would be rejected if others, both God and other Christians, knew my sin. I was convinced that the disclosure of my sins to fellow Christians would bring ridicule and rejection, and I couldn't face that. I didn't think that my heavenly Father looked upon me with compassion and love. And the spoken and unspoken message I heard in church was, "If you sin, you're a scumbag. This is a place for holy people." So though I felt miserable about it, I kept my mouth shut and tried to be "holy" like everyone else. (As I've grown older and wiser, I've discovered that everyone else had personal issues they were hiding too.)

Perhaps someone is treating you with condemnation. They may continue to throw your sin in your face with scorn. Perhaps you believe that what that person says is how your Lord feels toward you. And perhaps you think that's how all Christians feel toward you. But the Word of God makes it clear: There is one who loves you with a love that transcends your sin. He knows you are powerless against sin, and his love can lead you to deliverance.

There is incredible power in unconditional love—it's not abstract or ethereal, and it's not based on performance. When I hide my sin, I cut myself off from God's unconditional love and allow sin to grow in my life. When I hide my sin from another person, I'm saying, "Your love isn't big enough to handle my sin." Whether in our relationship with our Lord or in relationships with fellow Christians, we need to settle two facts in our minds. First, we need to know that their love for us is not diminished by our sin. And second, we need to know that our relationships with them are not in jeopardy because of our sin.

Is our Lord's unconditional commitment to you settled in both your mind and your emotions? Scripture tells us that the Spirit of God has poured his love into our hearts (Romans 5:5). And later in that same chapter, we are told that our Lord loved us when we were helpless, when we were sinners and when we were enemies (Romans 5:6, 8, 10). Only this unconditional love can free us from sin's deadly grip. As we rest in this secure love, sin begins to lose its attraction and its power to control our lives.

Quit sinning, or else! One of the saddest mistakes well-meaning Christian leaders make—particularly church leaders and parents—is to attempt to control sin in the lives of those they lead with rules and regulations. They fail to realize that such actions *ignite* sin instead of *eradicating* it. I remember going to youth camps where the first hour was spent in an orientation presenting all the rules that were to be obeyed. It never had the effect that was intended. For one thing, the Bible is very clear that "law" has a fascinating effect on sin. When rules, commandments or orders are given, they trigger sin's motivation to act and challenge the hearer to violate the rule.

I recall seeing a cartoon by Wiley Miller of a couple waiting to cross the street. A sign was posted that said, "No machete juggling allowed." The husband was looking at his wife and saying, "Suddenly I have an urge to juggle machetes." The cartoonist cleverly caught the spirit of this truth. When a rule is given, sin activates an urge within us to prove that no one can tell us what to do.

Our society seems to be very creative at coming up with laws to control people's behavior. Consider some of these:

• In the state of Missouri, it is illegal to play hopscotch on the sidewalks on Sundays.

• Hunting moths under streetlights is illegal in Los Angeles, California.

• In Muskegon, Michigan, it's against the law for a baseball player to hit a ball over the fence or out of the park.

• A hunting license is required to catch mice in Cleveland, Ohio.

• Growing dandelions within the city limits is against the law in Pueblo, Colorado.

• In Gary, Indiana, it's against the law to go to a movie theater within four hours of eating garlic.

Using laws and rules to free us from sin's grasp is a dead end. All our edicts, instructions and rules have no power to deliver us from sin's deadly grip. In fact, they motivate sin to greater persistence. Admonitions to read your Bible more, attend church more regularly and pray longer simply don't empower us. We must have something more powerful than rules to defeat this inner monster. The best motivation for dealing with sin is an intimate relationship with our loving Father. The power of unconditional love moves us to respond positively. And this is why laws and rules don't work. They don't lead us into an intimate relationship; they are merely external directives to perform more appropriately. No matter how diligently we try to suppress sin with good deeds, it's the wrong course of action and never fills our tank. Only love that is lavishly given as a free gift can do this. Nothing else works, because nothing else gets at the root problem.

Several years ago I conducted a wedding for a couple in my church. A few months following the wedding they came to my wife and me for counsel. As they sat with us in our living room, the husband said something like, "I'm about to explode! My emotional tank is almost empty from trying to do everything the way my wife wants it done. It seems as though that's the only way I can make her happy." He felt obligated to follow her rules in order for her to be satisfied with their relationship. During our time together, the wife came to see that she needed to love and accept her husband without placing her demands on him as a condition for the relationship. Because she had a teachable heart and a passion to honor Jesus Christ, she began to understand how to extend unconditional love. As the terms of their relationship changed, their level of intimacy increased.

Do you understand the life principle that is being outlined here? I'm saying that the power of God's love, poured out through the Holy Spirit who lives in us, draws us into intimacy with him. The knowledge and experience of this supernatural love is the only power sufficient to free us from sin's powerful grip. When the Bible talks about "walking in the Spirit," it is describing an ongoing relationship in which we live out this intimate communion with our Lord. A byproduct of this relationship is that sin loses its appeal because something a hundred times better has replaced it. This reality is available to you as a free gift from a loving Father.

The bottom line is that only our Lord is capable of dealing with the sin problem, and he does it by satisfying our inner hunger better than sin can. So when you sin, don't run away from the Lord in shame; run into his arms and tell him how much you need him to embrace you and meet your real need. Tell him that you are sick of being deceived and robbed by sin. Tell him that you hunger for him. Then believe that he hears the cry of your heart. Rest in his love.

The Bible demonstrates that only our Lord's transforming love is capable of creating the context in which we can find freedom. Nothing is as powerful as a passionate love relationship. People make incredible sacrifices with smiles on their faces and joy in their hearts because they are experiencing the reality of someone loving them unconditionally. They feel warm and secure. They feel a sense of freedom. They feel fulfilled. So with this dynamic at work in them, they are motivated to honor and serve the one who loves them so passionately, so purely, so completely.

Robert, a pastor in Nashville, was trying to train his Great Dane, Samson, not to wander off. He tried every means of training and control but to no avail. It seemed that every technique he tried only stimulated Samson's desire to outwit Robert. Then one day Robert's daughter, Hannah, said to him, "Dad, I know now what Samson's real problem is," and she proceeded to read an excerpt from a book she was reading:

In a dog's mind, a master or a mistress to love, honor, and obey is an absolute necessity. The love is dormant in the dog until brought into full bloom by an understanding owner. Thousands of dogs appear to love their owners, they welcome them home with enthusiastic wagging of the tail and jumping up, they follow them about their houses happily and, to the normal person seeing the dog, the affection is true and deep. But to the experienced dog trainer this outward show is not enough. The true test of real love takes place when the dog has got the opportunity to go out on its own as soon as the door is left open by mistake and it goes off and often doesn't return home for hours. That dog loves only its home comforts and the attention it gets from its family; it doesn't truly love the master or mistress as they fondly think. True love in dogs is apparent when a door is left open and the dog still stays happily within earshot of its owner. For the owner must be the be-all and end-all of a dog's life.[3]

What a graphic picture of the power of true love! What happens to the child of God whose heavenly Father becomes the be-all and end-all of life? Is it possible that sin remains attractive to you because you've not experienced the satisfying, passionate love of your heavenly Father? I'm not asking if you know the verses about how he loves you; I'm asking you if you know the *reality* of that love deep in your soul.

I've met lots of earnest, hard-working Christians. They diligently try to live upright lives. But when they are completely honest with me, they admit that they aren't enjoying the Christian life as much as they thought they would. I hear them say things like, "People think that I'm a godly Christian, but if they knew the real me they'd be surprised," or, "I try hard to please Jesus, but I'm always taking one step forward and two steps backward." They attempt to love him without first being overwhelmed by his love. They believe in the *fact* of his love, but they aren't enjoying the *experience* of that love.

God's Elite Squad

One thing that disturbs me is how rare this unconditional love is in most churches. If the head of our family—our beloved Father—is so kind and compassionate toward us when we are trapped in sin's power, why aren't the family members more like the Father? Why are we so frightened to admit our addictions to those who should love us unconditionally? Why does the church seem to be the last place where we want to admit that we need help? And when we do admit it, why are we often treated as though we've been put on probation? If unconditional love is the power that frees us, why aren't we more committed to share it with those around us? Why are we so afraid of another's sin?

I'm puzzled. We've been entrusted with the power to liberate others, and too often we use strategies that do the very opposite. We are so preoccupied with showing how perfect we are that our churches often reflect the image that we don't want sinners to attend. So sinners either hide their sin or leave. I wouldn't feel comfortable going to a doctor who criticized me for being ill!

We are called to be our Father's elite representatives, telling others about a love that defies definition. Jesus said, "By this everyone will know that you are my disciples, if you have love for one another" (John 13:35 NRSV). If we believe that our Lord loves us despite *our* sin, then as his family representatives we need to love others despite *their* sin.

Why don't we do this more powerfully and more consistently? I can think of at least four reasons.

First, we aren't convinced of our Father's unconditional love toward us, his children, trapped in patterns of sin. We get fed up with each other's issues and believe that's how our Lord feels about us.

Second, we are often afraid to deal with another's sin. We are afraid that we will be looked down upon and accused of being soft on sin. Sometimes we don't know what to do to help the sin problem, so we distance ourselves from the person.

Third, often we are not compassionate toward another's sin because we feel guilty about our own hidden issues. The guilt we feel gets projected onto others in the form of admonitions, rules and conditions. We fear that if we let people be honest about *their* sin, we'll have to face *our* sin.

Fourth, sometimes we reject others because we believe that we are better than they are. We are blind to our own nauseating sin of pride.

No biblical account illustrates this better than the account of the woman who was caught in adultery and brought to Jesus (John 8:1-11). The dignified, cultured religious leaders were using this incident to set Jesus up and find a reason to attack him. But the immediate issue was the punishment the woman would endure before the august religious assembly. It's interesting that the text says, "They made her stand before the group" (John 8:3). This is the ultimate act of shame and humiliation. Then they recited the law to condemn the woman and entrap Jesus. But he knew the evil that lurked in their hearts, and his response caught them off guard. As they prodded him for an answer, he replied, "Let anyone among you who is without sin be the first to throw a stone at her" (John 8:7 NRSV). This simple statement caused the accusers to slink away, vanishing with their guilt. Can you imagine the woman's emotional response to Jesus' words? He asked, "'Has no one condemned

you?' 'No one, sir,' she said. 'Then neither do I condemn you,'
Jesus declared. 'Go now and leave your life of sin'" (John 8:10-
11). The religious leaders' solution to the woman's sin was to
kill her. Jesus' solution was to extend forgiveness and offer her
a new life.

Time for a listening check. I've said that we, as recipients of
unconditional love, should be eager to share that love with
those around us. But loving others unconditionally doesn't
mean that we don't care about their sin. The Bible is clear that
we are to be people who hate sin—not sinners. Unconditional
love says, "I'm not here to condemn you or add more rules to
your life, but I do want to help you find our Lord's freedom
from sin." A person who has a biblical view of unconditional
love believes that the sinner is a child of God who is trapped
in a behavior that threatens life's fullness.

In my own experience I've found a few Christians who don't
care about how they live. But I've talked to many Christians
who say they have patterns of sin they can't conquer. When I
express compassion for their dilemma and offer to help them
find our Lord's solution, they are genuinely grateful and recep-
tive. The fact that someone expresses the compassionate heart
of our Lord gives the struggling Christian renewed hope that
there's an answer to his or her problem. This observation has
been tested for more than four decades of my life.

Applying the principle. I've said that until you experience a
relationship with someone who loves you despite your sin, you
will not find the freedom the Scriptures talk about. The one
person who *really* loves you in this way is your gracious heavenly Father. He is not disturbed about your sin; he is disturbed
that you are not allowing him to fill the void that prompts you
to sin. So let me suggest three ways you can begin to move
more solidly into this relationship of loving grace.

First, focus your attention on his passionate love for you *just as you are*. He knows you don't have the power within yourself to defeat sin. That power will come from your relationship with him. So doesn't it make sense to concentrate on getting to know the depths of his love for you? Unconditional love means that your relationship is not conditioned on your being sinless—that would be a hopeless situation. Our loving Father is very gracious. Jesus affirms our secure position when he says, "My Father, who has given them to me, is greater than all; no one can snatch them out of my Father's hand" (John 10:29). The writer of Hebrews reminds us that God has said, "Never will I leave you; never will I forsake you" (Hebrews 13:5). When we know someone loves us unconditionally, joy and peace invade our hearts and minds. We begin to live with an inner tranquility, which brings delight to our souls. The apostle John urges us to "see how very much our heavenly Father loves us, for he allows us to be called his children, and we really are!" (1 John 3:1 NLT).

Second, seek out another person who will love you unconditionally, and let that person in on your struggle. Gifted individuals can be channels through which the Holy Spirit expresses his wisdom and power. An even more ideal situation is to become part of a group committed to being a compassionate support network for each other. All of us need a safe place where we can openly process the issues that control us. I have found such groups invaluable because they are containers where the love of Christ can be experienced.

I participate in two such groups for my own growth, so I can speak from firsthand experience. One is a group of six to eight men who meet every other Thursday morning at 6:00 a.m. with coffee cups in hand. The group started about two years ago when Mark, our leader, asked us to make a one-year commitment to build our friendships and encourage and support each other. We agreed that our Thursday mornings together would be a time when we could be transparent and vulnerable, not fearing condemnation. Anything can be put on the table because we agreed that what is shared will be held in confidence. Because the leader modeled openness and vulnerability, men began to be honest about their personal struggles with sin. Individuals don't have to feel alone when they are a part of groups like this.

Third, commit not to hide your sin. A support person or group such as I've mentioned above should be trustworthy enough for you to share the issues that defeat you. One of the most basic principles for finding our Lord's plan of deliverance is to get the sin issues out in the open. *Hidden sin always grows.* Determine not to let that happen no matter how scary it is to confess your sin. I'm not suggesting an indiscriminate broadcasting of our issues, but among trusted, loving friends, we should be able to find a place of safety.

Making It Personal

1. Read through the Psalms, making note of what they tell you about your heavenly Father. Write down specific verses that tell you how much he loves you, and frequently meditate on them.

2. Begin to pray for our Lord's guidance in bringing an individual or individuals into your life who are trustworthy and compassionate. Look for him to answer that prayer.

3. How would you define unconditional love? Can you describe someone you know who expresses it?

5

LIVING IN
NO MAN'S LAND

*"As health expels disease,
and light swallows up darkness,
and life conquers death,
the indwelling of Christ through the Spirit
is the health and light and life of the soul."*
ANDREW MURRAY

*"In the same way,
count yourselves dead to sin
but alive to God in Christ Jesus."*
ROMANS 6:11

After I'd been a Christian for many years, I realized that I was living with a misconception about the Christian life. I didn't like being manipulated, shamed and defeated by sin in my life. I wanted to tell Satan, "Leave me alone. I want peace and quiet, but you won't let that happen because you're a pain in the neck." At the same time, I wasn't willing to commit myself to a life wholly devoted to our Lord. In my mind, that life was one of harsh sacrifices with little enjoyment. I feared that if I cast myself on him, he'd make me do everything I dreaded.

So what I tried to do was live in a neutral zone. That way I wouldn't be harassed by the evil one, but I also wouldn't have to be sold out to Jesus. I guess I thought that I could live my own life and not offend either Christ or the devil. If Switzerland could claim neutrality in World War II, why couldn't I do the same in my world? Then I wouldn't have to be anyone's enemy. I could live in peace while they went on with their fights. After all, at heart, I'm a man of peace, and I could model that for the world!

 ***Principle #4:** The more my relationship to Christ thrives, the more sin loses its power to manipulate my flesh.*

But this balloon was popped the day I discovered there is no such thing as neutrality in the Christian life. Thinking that I could be on the fence was pure illusion.

We are either for God or against him; there is no demilitarized zone between the opposing forces. The positive outcome of my discovery was that it made me see where I really wanted to stand and with whom I wanted to be identified. My tendency is to sneak away from conflict and hide in the bushes, but I was forced to declare whose team I'm really on. I had to decide whether I'd be a wholehearted or halfhearted participant in the Christian life.

Then I gained a second insight as I began to reorder my private world. The truth was obvious, but I hadn't seen it with the clarity I now had. I realized I couldn't move into a new position without leaving an old position. I gained this perspective one day while I was mediating on Romans 6:11. Paul writes, "In the same way, count yourselves dead to sin but alive to God in Christ Jesus." I wanted to be free from sin's irritating power to manipulate and dictate my mind and body. And as I pondered Paul's words, I realized that the Bible teaches what I call the Principle of Inverse Relationship regarding sin. I began to see that finding freedom from sin is inseparably connected to our view of and experience with our Lord. We never deal with sin in isolation. But sadly many of us become so preoccupied with sin's harassment and the shame it produces that we neglect to cultivate the delivering power. We ignore the source of our strength and muddle along in our weakness, failure and discouragement. No wonder defeat is our middle name.

We can never deal with sin effectively in isolation. As I continued to grapple with our Lord's strategy for dealing with sin in our lives, I began to see the principle in Romans 6:11 expressed in other places in the Bible. My mind flashed back to the time when the Jews made their exodus from Egypt. Our Lord brought them out of bondage and slavery and into a place of freedom, joy and abundance. The intermediate forty years of wandering in the wilderness demonstrated that merely leaving Egypt was not an adequate solution. The wilderness was not a fulfilling experience. They were brought out of Egypt's oppression to be brought into a land that flowed with milk and honey. The wilderness experience was wearisome, unsatisfying and joyless because it was not our Lord's intended place for his people. Living halfway between heaven and hell proved to be no picnic for the Israelites.

I also see this Principle of Inverse Relationship in Jeremiah's writings. In Jeremiah 2:13 our Lord, speaking through the prophet, says, "My people have committed two sins: They have forsaken me, the spring of living water, and have dug their own cisterns, broken cisterns that cannot hold water." Why would a person do such a senseless thing? Doesn't that seem rather stupid? But before we badmouth the Israelites, we need to recognize that we're often no different in our actions. When we are not fully satisfied with our heavenly Father and his abundant provisions, we begin to search high and low for a substitute. We know his words are true—our efforts leave us unfulfilled, like a sieve that water runs through unhindered—

but often we blindly blunder along, trying this and that but never finding satisfaction for our hearts.

Lloyd, a friend of mine, was such a person. For over thirty years he said, "I'm a follower of Jesus Christ. I've trusted him as my Savior." But one day he realized that he experienced no spiritual power and intimacy with our Lord. For thirty years his lips said, "I love Jesus," but his life said, "I don't believe you, Lord." Though he heard God's truth, he never acted on it. He'd never responded to what our Lord said regarding the use of his possessions. He'd never acted on what the Bible taught about healthy, loving relationships with his wife and family. What he professed and what he did simply didn't match. But the day this truth hit him, he realized his life needed to turn around. If you met Lloyd today, he would tell you that his life now is more vibrant and fulfilling.

The nature of sin is to cut us off from the only source that can empower and satisfy us. We saw this in the serpent's original approach to Eve. His basic strategy was to alienate Eve from her Creator and power source so she would be at the mercy of the evil one's manipulation. Tragically, he maneuvered her into his corner, seduced her and then took control of her life. That dominion is more powerful than a python's muscles squeezing life out of its victims. Unless we appropriate a power greater than ourselves, we're finished.

Perhaps you've noticed that sin replaces joy, peace and strength in our lives with fear, shame and guilt. And what do these emotions cause us to do? *We hide* (Genesis 3:10*).* And from whom? *Our source of life.* That's why our heavenly Father's first step in our deliverance is to remove the basis for our fear, shame and guilt. His beloved Son's death in our place provided a way for these three alienating issues to be discarded once and for all. He provided a way for us to come boldly before God to receive the grace, love and mercy we so desperately need.

We are told plainly in the Word of God, "There is now no condemnation for those who are in Christ Jesus, because through Christ Jesus the law of the Spirit of life set [us] free from the law of sin and death" (Romans 8:1-2). Reread these verses with this question in mind: What is it that sets me free from sin's oppressive control? Answer: *The life of Jesus Christ released through the Spirit of God who lives inside of you.* It is necessary for us to understand that our loving Lord never intended for us to live under the dominion of sin. Whatever your present experiences are, you need to settle this point. He does not leave us destitute to be harassed, bullied and beaten down by sin.

Our Lord's Flawless Solution

So what is our Lord's answer to sin, according to Romans 6:11 and 8:1-2? First, notice that Paul says we can *"count [ourselves] dead to sin."* That word *count* is an important word. Paul uses it thirty-five times in his epistles. The word in the original language was often used in secular documents relating to accounting and numerical calculations, like counting data in a ledger. Kenneth Wuest quotes an early example of this type of usage: "Put down to one's account, let my revenues be placed on deposit at the storehouse; I now give orders generally with regard to all payments actually made or credited to the government."[1]

The word expresses a settled decision based on facts. R. C. H. Lenski wrote, "The verb does not mean 'to conclude' in a mere logical fashion but 'to reckon' with certain facts as facts *so as to act on them because they are facts.*"[2] The Word of God clearly teaches that the authority sin had over us was broken when

Jesus Christ died on our behalf. We have no obligation to sin, and sin has no authority over us. We are now called to agree with the biblical facts and count ourselves dead to sin's enslaving power.

But that's only step one. We won't find freedom until we take step two and count ourselves alive to God in Christ Jesus. What does this mean practically? Well, remember we said earlier that people in their natural state have no strength to cope with the power and cunning of sin. To count ourselves alive to another indicates that a relationship has been established and that we can move into that relationship with freedom, joy and anticipation. We can draw upon the strength of that relationship. Relationships can empower us, or they can drain our life and leave us feeling weak. When we are experiencing a growing relationship with Christ, we gain his strength to stand against the pressures of sin. We enjoy God's company, relate freely and find strength in our interactions with him. In step one, the authority of sin over us has been broken. We no longer owe sin any obligation. But if we stop there, we'll be disappointed because we have not moved into the life-giving relationship with God for which we were created.

Jesus described this with a helpful illustration. He told a story about a demonic spirit that was dwelling inside a man and destroying his life. The man was forced to obey the demands of this evil monster. Then one glorious day, he was delivered from the oppressor's tyranny. He was free; his life was swept clean and put in order. But because no power replaced the evil spirit in the man's life, the spirit returned with seven other evil spirits, and conditions for the man were worse than before (Matthew 12:43-45).

Now in this chapter we have not been talking about evil spirits, but Jesus' illustration reminds us that the purpose of his deliverance is to create a home for his presence. When we're granted freedom from sin's domination, if we don't replace it with a growing relationship with our heavenly Father, we haven't gained the life-giving power that enables us to resist sin. When Satan or his cohorts knock at the door and we answer, he knows that he can outmaneuver us and trick us into sinning. Although his right to control us has been taken away, he still claims an illegitimate authority. But when our Lord answers the door and says, "You aren't welcome here any longer. Beat it!" the enemy knows his scam won't work, and he leaves. (But he returns periodically just in case we open the door to him.)

So the question we have to answer is, What, or who, replaces the power of sin in our lives? When this evil monster rules over us, we develop feelings of shame, guilt and defeat. When our Lord knocks at our door and wants to establish an intimate relationship with us, we are sometimes uncomfortable because the negative emotions are still present. And the negative emotions insist that we be cautious about letting *anyone* in—especially our Lord. It's even worse if we perceive God as harsh and judgmental. But we need to recognize that God has made peace with us and that we can't listen to our fear, shame and guilt. We need the courage and conviction to welcome our Lord with open arms. Cultivating this vibrant, close friendship with our Lord is an essential element in dealing with patterns of sin.

What does all this mean for us? It reminds us that we shouldn't constantly focus our attention on patterns of sin or how we get delivered. *Preoccupation with sin is a misdirected focus.* Rather we need to concentrate our attention and energy on our delightful and freeing relationship with our heavenly Father. We learn to enjoy him and discover that he enjoys being with us. Basically the more we enjoy him and his presence, the more sin loses its power in our lives.

As I write these words, I'm reminded of how many of us struggle to keep our weight under control. We've tried the Atkins diet, the cabbage diet, the Ormish diet and the grapefruit diet and still feel bloated. We're always weight conscious, measuring ourselves against some model or athlete. Food takes up so much of our focus that we don't enjoy life. When this happens, we've lost the heart of what life is about and don't like who we are. In a similar manner, sin can become our obsession—it's all that we see.

I have to add this point: many people feel awkward, shy or frightened at the thought of an intimate relationship with our beloved heavenly Father and Jesus Christ. Perhaps they have grown up with cold, harsh, and demanding adults and have come to believe that our Lord is like that. Even when they hear or read that God loves them, they can't assimilate these truths on the emotional level. Thus they acknowledge the truth, but it has little or no practical effect on their daily life experience. A process must be initiated to allow the truth to change the emotional response.

Perhaps if I describe how such a process worked in my life, you can adapt it to your situation. Early in my Christian life, I came to believe that even though my heavenly Father had honored the death of his Son, Jesus, on my behalf, he really didn't like me. It felt as though he was saying, "Wakefield, why don't you get your act together? Do you realize what a disappointment you are to me? Get with it!"

Then one day I began reading through the Psalms, cataloging each verse that told me something about my heavenly Father. The process of gaining what I call a profile of my heavenly Father was powerful in reshaping my view of who he is and how he feels about me. But those nagging feelings that he didn't like me prevailed. So I chose one verse that had come to mean a lot to me, and I committed it to memory. Psalm 145:8 says, "The Lord is gracious and compassionate, slow to anger and rich in love."

Then I made the decision that whenever I felt what I perceived to be God's feelings of rejection and disappointment, I'd speak to him in the following manner: "Father, I feel as though you are angry [or whatever emotion I was experiencing] with me. But the Bible says you are gracious and compassionate, slow to anger and rich in love. Now I recognize my feelings but choose to believe what the Bible says."

I adopted the strategy of choosing to believe God rather than my feelings. As I consistently applied this practice, a process began to take effect in my life; it slowly but genuinely changed my feelings.

But There's Still More Available

Whatever our Lord does, he does with great generosity. He is a superabundant provider. As if knowing him as a beloved friend were not enough, he has also made a practical provision to strengthen us against evil. He has placed us in a spiritual family with a powerful, unconditional love. One of the most practical ways I've felt this love is through the small support groups that I mentioned in chapter four.

Looking back over the more than a half century I've known Jesus Christ as my Savior and Lord, I realize how invaluable it would have been if I had belonged to a safe, caring group that would have nurtured my growth from the start. As far back as my teen years, I can see how desperately I needed loving men with whom I could share my secret sins. But I was scared to death that if they knew me they'd reject me. So my sin issues

were always kept underground, where they grew abundant
crops. But remember, I needed more than just a safe place to
seek help with patterns of sin—*I needed a place to be loved
unconditionally.* I am grateful that in recent years I have found
a fellowship of men who are learning to relate to each other in
this way.

I am troubled by the number of church leaders I know who
never model the kind of transparency and vulnerability I'm
describing. Many of them don't make an effort to gather men
and women into same gender groups where wise and loving
support is extended to those who want to find freedom. My
personal experiences, as well as my conversations with hundreds of men and women, demonstrate that every Christian
needs this kind of mutual support and encouragement. For
example, as a seminary professor and leader in my church, I
have contact with large numbers of men. I am amazed at the
percentage of men who have some significant area of their life
in which they are experiencing a high-level temptation. And far
too many are coping alone—and failing. I have no doubt that
women are in the same situation.

Most of us attend our churches on a consistent basis. But
sadly, few of us find environments of grace and truth in which
we feel secure, loved and strengthened. Too often we are in
settings where we are merely being preached at. I'm not saying
that preaching itself is a bad thing. But I find that men and
women hunger for intimacy where the presence of Christ
brings transparency and vulnerability with one another. This is
the kind of setting in which the leader is as vulnerable as the
group members. I have observed that when people get a clear
understanding of God's provisions for sin and can apply this in
supportive relationships, the power of sin in their lives begins
to diminish. Sometimes just learning from each other's lives

helps. Sometimes it's the comfort of another's encouragement. Sometimes it's laying hands on someone and praying for our Lord's provision, protection or love. When we are serious about opening up to one another and our Lord, he will give us his help.

I never cease to be amazed at how our Lord coordinates my speaking and writing opportunities with life events. Just yesterday I sat in a room with four other men who love Jesus Christ and endeavor to honor him daily. We invited one man, who is in a place of powerful pastoral influence, to join us because we knew he was going through a season of incredible difficulty. He has sacrificially given of himself to others for many years, and now he is emotionally and spiritually depleted. His condition is not the result of a moral breakdown but the consequence of the stress and pressure of pastoral responsibilities. He is extremely vulnerable to the whispers of the evil one. He could easily respond to the subtle seduction of sin in his flesh and make a disastrous choice that would lead to defeat and heartache.

Our friend recognized he was in a safe place with us. He felt free to share the disturbing thoughts and feelings with us. We extended our love, support and care in tangible ways. Then we gathered around him, laid hands on him and spent time praying for him and his wife. We plan to follow this with consistent time and support. I left with a clear sense that my friend knew how powerfully and richly he was loved by our Lord and the men who surrounded him, and that God would give him the power to deal with sin's tempting whispers.

Making It Personal

1. Do you identify with the idea of trying to live in the neutral zone?

2. Describe in your own words what it means to "count yourselves dead to sin."

3. Do you tend to be preoccupied with your sins? What does this preoccupation lead to?

4. What keeps you from a deeper intimacy with our Lord?

5. With whom are you transparent and vulnerable?

6

COPING WITH
A HOME INVADER

"Every time I see a movie in
which people are doing coke, I want it.
I can almost taste it in the back of my throat,
and I still love the taste.
You don't get over drugs; you don't ever fall out of love."
PATTI DAVIS

"As it is, it is no longer I myself who do it,
but it is sin living in me."
ROMANS 7:17

For several years my daughter Annette has had a baffling medical problem. At totally unpredictable times, she becomes sick to her stomach and vomits for several hours. Sometimes it occurs when she has had an exciting evening, and at first we thought it was the result of heightened emotions or a nervous stomach. But then we observed that she gets ill even when there is no apparent emotional event activating it. Her doctor prescribed one medication, but it didn't bring any relief. An ultrasound indicated there was no problem with her gall bladder. Someone suggested that taking Dramamine might solve the problem, but this too has not been the remedy. At the time that I'm writing this, a specialist is planning to put a scope in her stomach to see if he can find any clues.

Somewhere in Annette's system is a culprit causing her an

uncomfortable and annoying problem. It rears its head every week or two then vanishes from sight, lying dormant until it wants to harass her with another miserable night of vomiting. Buried somewhere in her body is a root problem that exposes itself with a night of distress. Until the hidden source is found, the best the treatments can do is ease her discomfort. We can clearly see the symptom, but can't find the source of the problem.

Principle #5: Sin is the power; sinning is the symptom.

Sin Is a Noun, Not a Verb

Annette's exasperating medical condition is a helpful parable of our equally irritating spiritual condition. We become distressed or discouraged when we sin. We decide on a remedy such as the willful decision "I'm not going to do that again." But sadly we find our solution doesn't cure the problem. So we change our prescription to "memorize a Bible verse that tells me not to do that." But the dose of memorization doesn't bring permanent relief either. So we go to our spiritual "doctor," our pastor or spiritual mentor, for a thorough examination. After listening to our symptoms and checking our spiritual pulse, our pastor tells us, "You need to pray more. Remember, prayer changes things." So we renew our commitment to prayer but are discouraged when we find that this too doesn't cure our disease. All our good intentions don't resolve our dilemma because *we are attacking the symptom, not the source.* Like Annette's hidden culprit, our spiritual culprit hides beneath the surface, creating havoc.

I found help from the apostle Paul. The insightful apostle

pointed out that our problem is not sinning, but sin. He uses the word *sin* forty-one times but only once as a verb. Sin as a verb describes a behavior or action that we undertake. But a noun (as you may recall from English 101) is a "person, place or thing." So Paul reminds us that a powerful and aggressive agent is at work in us and its presence is revealed in our acts of sin. We need to concentrate our energy on the secret agent who is calling the shots behind the scene rather than exhaust ourselves on the overt actions. If we deal with the secret agent, we'll stem the symptoms more effectively.

We can trace the roots of this issue clear back to Genesis where we find Adam and Eve's son, Cain, angry because his offering was not accepted by our Lord. God's words to Cain are, "If you do what is right, will you not be accepted? But if you do not do what is right, *sin is crouching at your door; it desires to have you, but you must master it"* (Genesis 4:6, italics added). What is this thing that is crouching ready to spring into action and attack Cain?

It's the apostle Paul who most clearly identifies the insidious culprit who has invaded our personal space and raised internal havoc. He makes some startling statements. For example, he clearly identifies sin as an active, contentious force that has usurped control over our body. Read his sobering words in Romans:

- "We know that the law is spiritual; but I am unspiritual, *sold as a slave to sin"* (Romans 7:14).
- "As it is, it is no longer I myself who do it, but *it is sin living in me"* (Romans 7:17).
- "Now if I do what I do not want to do, it is no longer I who do it, but it is *sin living in me* that does it" (Romans 7:20).
- "But I see another law at work in the members of my body, waging war against the law of my mind and *making me a pris-*

oner of the law of sin at work within my members" (Romans 7:23).

I italicized some words to show Paul's constant emphasis. Notice that Paul identifies sin as a powerful force that exerts authority over our body's desires and lures us into overt acts of sin. *Vine's Expository Dictionary of Biblical Words* defines sin as "a governing principle or power, e.g., Romans 6:6, '[the body] of sin,' here 'sin' is spoken of as an organized power, acting through the members of the body, though the seat of 'sin' is in the will (the body is the organic instrument); in the next clause, and in other passages as follows, this governing principle is personified."[1]

For too many years I believed that my sinful behaviors were the result of my being a weak Christian, my inability to say no to temptation, unhealthy thinking or noxious patterns that I'd learned as a child. Although the enemy is quick to exploit these, now I know that the real problem is the underground power that has made its home in my "flesh," or my humanity apart from Christ's redemptive work. This ungodly force has gained control over my flesh and is able to dictate actions that I cannot resist with my own strength. It's impossible for me to match strength against this evil force that lives in my humanity. Face it, if you try to go into the ring with sin, you'll get knocked flat on your fanny.

Our spiritual counselors often tell us that we can overpower this evil dictator. Too often Christian leaders' solutions to the sin problem are "Try harder," "Read your Bible and pray more," "Say no to temptation" and so on. But these are no match for the power of sin, which can quickly short-circuit the mind, inflame our passions and initiate destructive behavior within us. Addiction comes in many forms and disguises, and all of us have experienced something that has an addictive hold on our lives. The majority of you reading this probably know what I am talking about. In our own selves we are defenseless against the evil force within us. So let's settle the issue: Trying harder isn't going to solve the problem. Until you are convinced that the answer to your sinning problem does not lie in your good intentions, resolutions and strivings, you will never find relief.

And don't think that you can bluff this internal tyrant. Unless you have access to a far greater power than this force, you'll never be able to bring it under control. It doesn't respond to reason, threats or pleading. It only responds to an authoritative force greater than itself, and that person isn't you or me. Thankfully there is a greater power to which sin *must* yield.

The Great Impostor

The Bible teaches us that Satan is the greatest deceiver in the universe. We are told that he "masquerades as an angel of light" (2 Corinthians 11:14). Like a chameleon, he can transform himself into whatever is required to catch us off guard and draw us into his clutches like a spider trapping a fly. It's important to notice that the Scripture mentioned above informs us that he can present himself as an "angel of light." He can appear as the epitome of goodness, the one who empathizes with you over your trying conditions. But keep in mind that he is the great impostor.

Now wouldn't it make sense that the ungodly power, sin, would follow the same strategy as Satan does? The sin living in our flesh is an impostor that will adapt itself to fool the one it wants to capture. This fraud knows you like a book. It is able to adapt itself to any situation to lure you into sin. Sin dwelling in the flesh is incredibly clever in convincing us that we need to sin to be fulfilled. How long would it take for you to list the ways that you have been conned into acts of sin that you later regretted? How many times have you fallen for the warm, beckoning voice that promises pleasure and fulfillment? How many times have you given in like the proverbial ox being led to the slaughter? How many times have you said, "I'll never do that again," only to succumb to its charms the next time. The writer of Proverbs described this happening to a young man caught in the clutches of an alluring but immoral woman:

> With persuasive words she led him astray;
>   she seduced him with her smooth talk.
> All at once he followed her
>   like an ox going to the slaughter,
> like a deer stepping into a noose
>   till an arrow pierces his liver,
> like a bird darting into a snare,
>   little knowing it will cost him his life. (Proverbs 7:21-23)

The Bible tells us that this evil, seductive energy called sin set up housekeeping in our flesh from our birth (Psalm 51:5). We are not told of its substance; rather we are informed of its reality and given abundant illustrations of how it shapes, corrupts and destroys who our Lord intended us to be in his original plan. Throughout the Bible we see person after person who showed great promise and was given great opportunities, but this inner presence wrought havoc and led the person to profound pain, sadness and loss. Whenever I think of Samson, I feel a sense of sadness that this man who knew God's strength consumed his life with lustful passion that ultimately destroyed him. The power of sin controlled his life and destroyed the person whom he had the potential to become. And even David, one of the greatest kings of Israel, seemed to be ruled by a passion that filled his later years with grief. You and I are no different. This evil presence has been a tenant in our lives from birth. It has shaped our habits, our emotional tone and our patterns of thinking. And it threatens to destroy us.

If we are going to find our Lord's strategy for dealing with sin, we must recognize this invisible yet powerful presence in our flesh. And we must acknowledge that in ourselves—that is, in our flesh—we are at the mercy of this power. We do not have the physical strength, the emotional stamina or the mental skill to overpower this indwelling enemy. Until I gave up all hope that I could overpower or outwit sin in my flesh, I lived a life of repeated defeat. The day I recognized that my Lord wasn't asking me to solve this problem, I sighed a huge sigh of relief. I finally understood that someone else would be the deliverer as soon as I got out of the way and let him take over.

Giving Sin a Green Light

Though we acknowledge that sin effectively camouflages itself and behaves in a deceitful manner, we do know something about the conditions under which it thrives. For one thing, the Bible tells us that *sin thrives in darkness*. The writer of Proverbs tells us of individuals who "leave the straight paths to walk in dark ways" (Proverbs 2:13). Jesus said, "Light has come into the world, and people loved darkness rather than light because their deeds were evil" (John 3:19 NRSV). The apostle Paul puts it this way: "Have nothing to do with the fruitless deeds of darkness, but rather expose them" (Ephesians 5:11). Each of the writers cautions us about the danger of keeping sin hidden in the dark. When we do this, we are playing into its hand, allowing it to gain strength and setting ourselves up to be overpowered.

Alex is an example of someone who kept his sin hidden. He had graduated from Bible college and was on the staff of a

church. One day he asked to meet me for a coke. As we sat
across from each other, Alex fiddled nervously with his drink.
Finally he blurted out, "I've got a problem with pornography
that no one else knows about. I can't control it. It's killing me,
and I need your help. Can we talk about it?" He finally realized
that he'd never get free from its clutches unless he could
openly talk about it with someone else.

Over the years I've discovered that most people want to tell
someone if they have an overpowering sin in their life, but the
fear of ridicule, condemnation or rejection is too powerful. The
nature of my ministry is such that countless individuals have
confided their hidden sins to me. The incredible thing is that
when they find a safe place to dump the internal crud, the
power of sin is weakened. It has a more difficult time thriving
when exposed to the light.

Reading *The Wounds of God,* a novel by Penelope Wilcock
about men living in a monastery during the Middle Ages,
reminded me of this principle. The abbot, Father Peregrine,
speaks with Brother Francis about his seemingly constant light-
heartedness. He believes that it is just a façade hiding something deeply rooted in his life. During the conversation, the
wise, godly abbot ponders these thoughts to himself:

> I can't get near this young man. . . . He has made himself a
> fortress. Amusing, courteous, responsible, but too well-
> defended for his own good. Father Matthew's right, there is
> something about this eternal cheerfulness . . . a rebuff . . . no,
> maybe not. Maybe he is protecting something . . . a wound
> somewhere.[2]

Then, under the abbot's gentle probing, Brother Francis's
protective shell begins to crack. The power of buried emotions
begins to surface:

His smile was gone suddenly, and the surface of his face was distressed with little twitches of nervous muscles that didn't know what to do now they were no longer employed in guarding his soul with the shield of a smile. "I have studied and practiced and done my utmost to please, but it is never enough. I am hemmed in by rebuke and censure until it seems there is nowhere left to stand. There is no place for me. I can never be good enough." The words tumbled out and stopped abruptly. Quivering in the unaccustomed exposure, he looked at the abbot, his brown eyes full of distress.[3]

The sad reality is that most churches encourage us to keep our sins in the closet. During my teens and twenties, I longed to find help with my struggle with sexual lust. But the last place I'd dare expose it was with church leaders. I was convinced that I'd face their wrath. Now I realize that each of them had their own hidden issues, but back then I believed that they were the epitome of purity and perfection. Only when we are convinced that we are in a safe place do we dare expose that practice that defeats and shames us. The message of every church should be, "This is a safe environment in which you can bring the issue that's defeating you into the open." We need to be saying, "This is an environment saturated with our Father's grace, and you will find compassion, hope and guidance as you face the problem of sin within you."

We know that sin thrives under law. I spoke of this in chapter four, but I refer to it here because it is such an essential characteristic of how sin can exploit good things. Paul's writings make this very clear. He says to the Roman Christians, "But sin, seizing the opportunity afforded by the commandment, produced in me every kind of covetous desire" (Romans 7:8), and "For sin, seizing the opportunity afforded by the commandment, deceived me, and through the commandment put me to death" (Romans 7:11). Whenever we set our own rules or try to follow those established by well-meaning Christians, we will only be creating a situation that triggers that inward desire to violate the rule.

This truth revealed itself in a comical way the other night. Winnie and I are in a small group that meets once a month for encouragement, support and laughter. This month we were having a White Elephant gift exchange. The idea is that each person wraps up some ugly, comical or worn out "treasure" that will be exchanged during the evening. The gifts are unwrapped one at a time with lots of laughter at the silly, creative or worthless items that have been given.

Winnie and I were hosting the evening in our home, and just prior to the unwrapping I said, "Remember, take home whatever gift you get. I don't want the junk left here." After the unwrapping, we had refreshments, and everyone enjoyed conversation with each other. Then people left. Only later did we discover that a couple of mischievous individuals had cleverly hidden most of the white elephant gifts around our house. My rule that they take their presents with them had prompted the impish response, "We'll creatively show you that we don't intend to follow your command!"

I recall reading about a waterfront hotel that had a sign posted saying, "Fishing is not allowed from the second-floor balcony." Yet guests were constantly observed casting their lines from the balcony into the water below. Finally someone suggested that the sign be taken down. When that occurred, people stopped fishing from the balcony. The prohibition had prompted people to prove that they could get away with it.

Sin Thrives on Feelings of Guilt and Worthlessness

Such emotions cause us to alienate ourselves from others and make it difficult for us to be open and vulnerable—even with people who love us. The loneliness, guilt and worthlessness then cause us to turn inward for satisfaction, and we inevitably turn to unhealthy ways, or sin, to fill the valid need. Thus the vicious cycle keeps repeating itself as we spiral downward, heaping one defeat upon another.

As a result of these conditions, sin creates habit patterns and addictions that deepen our dependency on the false hopes sin promises. As the dependency grows stronger, we become enslaved to the clutches of sin's ruthless power. We hate what is happening to us, but we are powerless to break out of sin's enslaving demands. Sin first approaches us as a caring friend, but it ends up being a tyrant who demands what he wants. Our flesh has become addicted to sin.

As I am writing this chapter, the news media is highlighting the drug addiction of a popular movie actor. In an article assessing the actor's condition, Patti Davis, the daughter of President Ronald Reagan, describes her own love affair with drugs. She portrays its incredible power with the following words:

> I knew a girl whose lover came in several disguises—white cross Methedrine, orange triangles of Dexedrine, "black beauties," long white lines of coke. She followed her lover everywhere—into parking lots with strangers, into dark cars, into the shadows along steep mountain roads, into apartments that smelled like stale smoke and had three or four locks on every door. When her lover wasn't with her, she was left with her own terror of how to move through the world alone. She didn't know how to deal with people alone; she needed her partner, her other half. You need to know this about drugs:

unlike people, drugs don't judge you or look at you too closely, too intimately. They don't ask you to reveal yourself or confide your secrets. They just take you away—far away; they let you hide, which is what frightened people want to do.[4]

Your addiction may not be to drugs, but I find that everyone is controlled by something that cannot be broken. It may be something that is joked about, worried about or cried over, but it has a grip that cannot be broken. In the quietness of my own thoughts, I know that I have no power to break its bondage. It has become my lover and my master. And, sadly, it is keeping me from experiencing something far greater—the fullness of intimacy with my Lord. He doesn't love me less, but sin's addictive power siphons off the all-embracing sense of unity with my Lord.

I am reminded of a true account of a family that decided to purchase a foot-long Burmese python as a family pet. After eight years it had grown to eleven and a half feet and weighed in at eighty pounds. One day the family pet wound itself around the fifteen-year-old son, Derek, and suffocated him. The family pet had turned into a family killer. Sin is no less vicious than the python. At first its presence is inviting, novel and fun. Then it ups the stakes and calls us to a greater commitment. More and more, it sucks us into a state of dependency, all the while demanding a higher loyalty. One day we wake up to the fact that we are completely in its power. That's scary!

Facing the Facts About Sin

As I investigated the Scriptures and spent time digesting what they say, I discovered four significant facts about sin that helped me understand how it operates within my flesh. Now I am more attuned to how it will try to seduce me with its constant, clever messages.

First, I've come to see that *sinning is a symptom of a deeper need.* Remember what I said earlier—of the forty-one times Paul uses the word *sin,* only once does he use it as a verb. Forty times he uses it as a noun. What I discovered is that Paul is attacking the source of the problem and not getting sidetracked with the symptom. If you have an ache in your side, you might rub some liniment on it to take away the soreness. But if the ache is a disease in an internal organ, the liniment will have no value in dealing with the real problem. Since I've learned to look at the source of my sin problem and not the symptom, I have a far better handle on where to concentrate my energy.

The second insight that has been helpful is that *sin attaches itself to a valid need.* The strategy of the evil one is extremely clever. He knows what our valid needs are, and he knows that if he can convince us to meet those needs with a sin-filled response, he will be able to gain control over our lives in those need areas. We must guard against belittling valid needs. Learn to separate the valid need from the way that sin is exploiting it.

Sam and Sue haven't been married long. Both are working full-time jobs that often require overtime. Lately they've been coming home tired and irritable. They have little time for meaningful conversations and rarely have a fun, relaxing date. In very subtle ways, they are beginning to move away from the intimacy that brought them together. At the same time, Sam is working with an attractive, warm, cheerful young woman at his job. At first they simply talked about job-related issues, then they began to chat about more personal matters, and lately he finds himself drawn to her emotionally. And Sue seems less attractive, less understanding and less desirable.

Do you see that Sam's valid need for intimacy with his wife is being seduced by an invalid source? He finds himself thinking about how pleasurable it would be to get even closer to his workmate. He enjoys the satisfaction of sharing intimate thoughts and feelings with her. The python is growing up and beginning to slowly wind itself around Sam. If he doesn't wake up and see what is happening, his marriage will be destroyed and something precious inside Sam will die.

When sin attaches itself to a valid need and seems to feed it, we develop a dependency on sin, which soon becomes an addiction. We need to be honest about our needs. It's important that we don't discount them. Also, we need to discover God's valid ways to meet our valid needs.

The third truth we need to grasp about the nature of sin is that *sin acts as a clever but false love.* One of the primary definitions of sin in the Bible is "to miss the mark." It's as if I know that I'm supposed to aim the arrow at the bull's eye, but I find it more tempting to aim at a bull. Sin gets me to aim at the wrong target so that I don't discover my heavenly Father's appointed way to meet a legitimate need in my life. Instead I'm convinced by sin's whisper that there is an easier, more immediate and more satisfying way to hit the target. Only later do I discover that I was duped. What appeared to be a more fulfilling target never really met my need. But now I'm in a worse state.

As I write this I'm aware that it is easy to describe this process cognitively, but the whole process is much more subtle, more attractive and more promising in actuality. On paper I can't convey the feelings that accompany the false promise. I can't convey how loving sin sounds when it seems to show such empathy with our loneliness, our yearning for intimacy, our feelings of failure, and so on. Often sin approaches me like an understanding friend. Sin sympathizes with me about how unfair it is that my needs are not instantly met. It whispers how unjust it is that someone seems to have failed me and that our Lord seems to be totally silent about it.

I don't know how many times I've talked with single, young Christian women who are lonely for a special man in their life. Often they easily meet attractive, winsome young men who aren't Christians. They hear the quiet whisper, "He could fill that void of loneliness. Yes, he's not a Christian, but notice how friendly he is. You don't want to go through life alone do you? You're not getting any younger, and another nice man like him may never come along." The message doesn't cease. The appealing, persistent voice of sin never lets up.

Sometimes we are in situations where there doesn't seem to be a valid way to meet a need. We wait and wait, but our Lord doesn't seem to act. We've even heard that quiet voice that says, "He really doesn't care. If he did, he'd do something about your need. Why don't you step out on your own and do something. I've got several good ideas. He won't like it, but quit waiting for him, and let's do something about that need."

My fourth discovery about sin is that *sin undermines our confidence in a faithful, loving Father and his ability to meet these valid needs.* We've already seen this in the serpent's interaction with Eve in the garden. He smoothly drops hints that her Lord isn't the loving person of integrity she thinks he is. He hooks those barbs into her mind and buries them so deep that they'll never come out without surgery. He seems to be suggesting, "Eve, if you're ever going to be fulfilled, if you're ever going to become a significant person, you'll have to stop looking to that God of yours and let me help you achieve those goals. After all, I'm your *real* friend."

The strategy of this powerful force is to shift our attention away from the valid sources to meet our valid needs. First and foremost, we need to look to our loving, gracious and generous heavenly Father to meet our needs. He has made clear promises that he will never violate. Too often we listen to the lies that discredit his integrity and move us away from him rather than into his loving arms. Many of us grew up not trusting anyone, and we transfer our mistrust and self-protection onto this number-one relationship. We may continue doing the outward acts of a Christian, but inwardly we relate to our Lord with an extended hand that says, "God, keep your distance. I don't trust you anymore than I trust anyone. I'll let you know if I ever need you, and then I'll give you clear directions how, when and where you are to do what I want." So the need never gets met.

Making It Personal

1. How much of what I've shared with you in this chapter is clear in your mind?

2. Do you agree that you can never successfully cope with sin in your own strength?

3. What is the implication of seeing sin as a root problem within your flesh?

4. Read Romans 5—8, noting what is said about sin. Try to develop a clear biblical profile of its nature, actions and impact on the flesh.

5. Think through your relationships. With whom do you feel safe talking about patterns of sin in your life?

6. Has your focus been on your sin, or sins, as a power operating in your flesh? What difference has this distinction made in your struggle?

7. Have you been living by keeping rules? If so, what does this chapter challenge you to put in their place?

7

HELP! I'VE GOT A SPLIT PERSONALITY

"Sin is sovereign till sovereign grace dethrones it."
CHARLES H. SPURGEON

"And if Christ is in you,
though the body is dead because of sin,
yet the spirit is alive because of righteousness."
ROMANS 8:10 (NASB)

A couple of years ago I was invited to my friend Lalo's birthday party. He had moved to the United States from Bolivia several years ago and was still not completely proficient in English. One of the games his wife had planned for the party was to ask Lalo to identify the meaning of common English clichés. For example, he was asked to explain the meaning of phrases like, "He who hesitates is lost," "It's time to hit the road," "A bird in the hand is worth two in the bush," "Milk it or move it," "What's up, doc?" and "It's an ill wind that blows no good." Lalo was able to decipher the meanings of some, but with many he was completely in the dark. We laughed at his interpretations, but I came away reminded of how important language and the meaning of words are to us.

Language shapes relationships. Our lives are shaped by the

messages that are sent to us from the moment of our birth—and probably while we were in our mother's womb. But as enriching as language can be for relationships, it often confuses and misleads us. We are constantly bombarded with messages that have hidden meanings. Communications educator Marshall McLuhan called language "organized stutter." We pick up clichés and mannerisms that others have to decode. We often try to express our feelings by using thinking words, or we'll say, "I feel . . ." when we actually mean, "I think . . ." Several centuries before Christ, Hippocrates, the Greek physician, said, "The chief virtue that language can have is clearness, and nothing detracts from it so much as the use of unfamiliar words."[1]

Not long ago, a friend was telling me about a sermon he'd listened to the day before. He said, "The preacher said, 'Just take it to the cross.' I had no idea what I was to take to the cross, or how I'd do it." "Take it to the cross" sounds very spiritual, but the average Christian may not know what it means. Early in my Christian experience, I became aware that my Christian friends were using words to talk about the Christian life that left me confused and disturbed. I'd listen to my pastor or Bible teacher speak about the "victorious" Christian life and hear other terms that left me wondering, "What's that all about?" Because I was shy and insecure, I didn't want to appear stupid, so I'd keep my mouth shut and walk away puzzled about what they meant.

As I continued to grow in my Bible knowledge, I kept finding mysterious terms to describe the Christian life. I've mentioned earlier that an important part of my spiritual journey has been clarifying confusing terms and finding out how they are worked out in daily living. The journey from ignorance to clear understanding has taken many years, and I'm still in the learning process.

I was reminded of this fact the other night while teaching a seminary class. We were examining what the Bible says about "walking in the Spirit." One eager student kept prodding me with questions throughout the entire two-hour class period. His questions were good, and he displayed a keen appetite to know about this truth and how to apply it to his life. Following the class, the student said, "This is all new to me. I've never heard about this before." I walked away from the classroom vividly aware of how important it is for me to communicate biblical truth in as clear and relevant terms as possible.

Understanding Who I Am

For too many years I was in the dark about how our Lord created us and how sin operates within me. I'd already griped about my frustration with Bible teachers who used vague, undefined and meaningless terms. I wanted desperately to live a life that honored my Lord, but I couldn't find the elusive key that would unlock the door to the victorious Christian life. None that I found would fit the lock. So I continued to fumble and bumble along with my feelings of guilt because I was failing to live up to the measure of perfection that my teachers were urging me to attain.

But through the Holy Spirit's faithful leadership in my life, I continued to grow in my relationship with God. An important part of this growth process consisted of me coming to a clear understanding of how our Lord has put us together. A significant discovery came when I realized that as the apostle Paul dealt with the problem of sin, he consistently made a distinction between spirit and flesh. Because he is so deliberate in separating the two, we will profit by a closer look.

One of the heresies in the early church was Gnosticism. The Gnostics taught a dualism between body and spirit. They believed that the material universe was inherently evil and that the nonmaterial, or the spiritual, was good. They believed that Jesus Christ only appeared to be in human form, like a phantom. Salvation was achieved by being freed from the material. In the past, some Gnostics practiced flagellation of the flesh to punish it for its sinfulness.

But when our Lord created Adam, he was a beautiful creation: body, soul and spirit. Each part of who we are was designed purposefully by our Lord so that we would be an integrated whole. In no way do we believe that our flesh is evil or that it should be treated as less than a temple of the Holy Spirit (1 Corinthians 6:19-20). Our Lord created us to function as a unit, but in coming to grips with the sin issue, we need to keep in mind the distinction between spirit and flesh.

 Principle #6: *Sin invaded the flesh; God redeemed the spirit.*

In Paul's writing, he uses the Greek word *sarx* over ninety times. This word has been typically translated as *flesh*.[2] A close examination of Paul's writings reveals that he uses the word in three different ways. First, Paul uses the word over thirty-five times to refer to *that which is physical or related to the body*. For example, in Romans 2:28 he says, "For he is not a Jew who is one outwardly; neither is circumcision that which is outward in the flesh" (NASB). And in 1 Corinthians 15:39, he says, "All flesh is not the same flesh, but there is one of men, and another flesh of beasts, and another flesh of birds, and another of fish" (NASB). These verses are clearly using *flesh* to refer to the physical.[3]

A second grouping of verses uses the word when referring to the human race. In I Corinthians, Paul writes, "For consider

your calling, brethren, that there were not many wise according to the flesh, not many mighty, not many noble" (1 Corinthians 1:26 NASB). Or when he speaks to the Galatians, Paul
says, "To reveal His Son in me, that I might preach Him among
the Gentiles, I did not immediately consult with flesh and
blood" (Galatians 1:16 NASB). You will find that Paul uses *flesh*
in this manner about twenty-five times.[4]

Paul's third usage is of particular interest to us. He uses *sarx*
twenty-seven times to refer to sin's active presence within a
person's body. Most of these references are in Romans and
Galatians when he is teaching believers about how sin attaches
itself to our humanity and how our Lord intends to deal with
its presence and power. The following references, all from the
New American Standard Bible, are representative of this third
grouping:[5]

• "For while we were in the flesh, the sinful passions, which
were aroused by the Law, were at work in the members of our
body to bear fruit for death" (Romans 7:5). Notice that he identifies sin with the members of our *body*.

• "For I know that nothing good dwells in me, that is, in my
flesh; for the wishing is present in me, but the doing of the
good is not" (Romans 7:18).

• "For the flesh sets its desire against the Spirit, and the Spirit
against the flesh; for these are in opposition to one another, so
that you may not do the things that you please" (Galatians 5:17).

How Sin Interacts with Our Flesh

Several insights have helped me get a handle on where sin
attacks us. I have chosen to retain the word *flesh* because it is
difficult to use a more contemporary word without creating
more confusion. It's a word that needs to have its own unique
definition. We will be able to think through this more clearly if

we grasp the biblical use of the word and keep its precise definition of this aspect of who we are. For our discussion, it's
especially important to grasp the third way that Paul uses the
word. When he describes our flesh, he is speaking of *who we
are apart from the work of Christ* in our life. So the first insight
is that *our flesh is who we were before we were born again*. It
refers to our body, mind and emotions prior to our salvation.
After we were born again, the Holy Spirit gave our spirit life,
but the Scripture suggests that our flesh remained the same.

The second insight is that *sin has invaded our flesh*. Paul
makes this very clear in several passages in Romans where he
makes the following statements (again, all are from NASB):

• "I am of flesh, sold into bondage to sin" (Romans 7:14).

• "So now, no longer am I the one doing it, but sin which ind-
wells me" (Romans 7:17).

• "For I know that nothing good dwells in me, that is, in my
flesh" (Romans 7:18).

• "I am no longer the one doing it, but sin which dwells in
me" (Romans 7:20).

• "Making me a prisoner of the law of sin which is in my
members," (Romans 7:23) Notice again that he locates sin *in
his members*—his body.

In these passages, Paul is very consistent in demonstrating
that sin, as an active force, has somehow attached itself to our
flesh—our body, mind and emotions—with a grip that we cannot break in our own strength. He identifies sin as an issue of
our flesh, not our spirit. Note this point very carefully: He is
not saying that our flesh is evil; he is saying that evil has overrun our flesh. It has established a beachhead in the flesh.

It's not difficult to understand how this has happened. Earlier we noted that we were born into sin. I used the analogy of
being born with a sin gene that made us susceptible to sin's

infiltration and control of our flesh. Since we didn't have the Spirit of God within us to teach, guard and strengthen us, sin had no difficulty shaping our thinking, stroking our emotions and attaching itself to our physical desires. I often tell people that sin got the first crack at us and conditioned us to follow its lead. What I am especially concerned about is that you understand that sin is rooted in your flesh, *not* in your spirit. Understanding this distinction is crucial to knowing how our Lord intends to deal with the problem of sin.

Perhaps you have heard the term *total depravity?* Total depravity doesn't mean that we are sewer rats, perverts or the scum of the earth. Rather total depravity means that the power and control of sin have infiltrated every aspect of our flesh. The members of our physical body, our mind, our emotions, our will—all of these aspects of us have been penetrated by the presence of sin. A person can be an upright, honest, caring and dignified individual yet have every fiber of his or her being touched by sin's influence.

The third insight that I have discovered is that *the flesh is defenseless against the subtle infiltration of sin.* In a very real sense, it is helpless to cope with this bigger, cleverer bully. Let me refresh your memory—Adam and Eve were not created with an internal mechanism to fight sin. The Garden of Eden was a place of innocence. Think of it as a population that never contracted malaria because malaria was not in the environment. Personally, I have never contracted that disease, but it's not because I am *immune* to it, but because I have never been *exposed* to it. In like manner, when Adam and Eve were exposed to sin, they were vulnerable and fell victim to its clutches.

A fourth insight I found is that *when our Lord transforms us into new spiritual beings, this change doesn't change our flesh.*

I think many of us were misled into believing that when we responded to Jesus Christ we would become completely new, but we soon found that our flesh still wanted to follow those old patterns that were learned in sin. Sin still reigned in the flesh. Our Lord's strategy is not to eradicate the sin in our flesh at the time of our conversion, but to connect our spirit with the Spirit of God so that we have a new power that is competent to deal with the enemy in our flesh. Remember, there is a difference between our sins being completely forgiven and the presence of sin continuing in our flesh. At the point of salvation, when we trusted in the work of Jesus Christ and claimed him as our Savior, our flesh was not converted, but we became a new spiritual creation united with our Lord's own Spirit. Don't expect what isn't converted to act converted!

Separating Two Identities

Can you see why these two components have to be distinguished? You were born as a flesh being when you entered this world. That's your membership in the human race. There was nothing evil about you as a human being, but sin immediately set about to infiltrate you and permeate your mind with unwholesome thoughts, push your emotions out of control and stimulate bodily appetites to the point of addictions. Like the apostle Paul, you now find yourself doing the very things you don't want to do and not doing the things you'd like to do. And you're powerless to halt this force from ravaging you as a human being. You may be cultured, educated and disciplined, but because you were born in sin, your flesh is at sin's mercy—and sin isn't merciful!

The good news is that you became a new creation when you placed your faith in Jesus Christ. You became a new *spiritual creation* that is meant to be the counterpart to your flesh.

And this is the you that is connected with your heavenly Father and his Son, Jesus Christ. This is the you that has an eternal standing. Your flesh will one day be placed in a coffin or be burned to ashes in cremation, but the eternal you will not be touched by disease or death. This sinful person is not your core identity. We often speak of our identity in Christ. What we mean is that the Spirit of God has baptized us into his beloved Son and now he sees us as he sees his Son. He identifies us as one with the Lord Jesus. This is our core identity.

One of the most important aspects of this new you is the way your spirit has been connected to the Spirit of our Lord. The power to confront the sin in our flesh resides in this new, mighty, invincible power that has been bonded to our spirit. So now we can begin to understand our Lord's strategy. He doesn't change our flesh; rather he unites our spirit with a force that is greater than the evil force in our flesh. His intention is to defeat this persistent power by bringing a new greater power through our spirit. A crucial key is to discover how to join forces with the Spirit of God in a way that allows his unlimited power to be unleashed against the enemy that occupies our flesh.

In a sense, this is not about you; it is about the internal power of sin in your flesh and the internal power of the Spirit in our spirit. Can you now see why Paul reminds the Galatian Christians that "the flesh sets its desire against the Spirit and the Spirit against the flesh; for these are in opposition to one another" (Galatians 5:17 NASB)? He is using the word *flesh* here to mean that place where sin is in control, prompting us to ungodly thoughts, feelings and actions.

The Old Testament has a beautiful picture of this process. Our Lord promised Abraham that his descendants would dwell in a land flowing with milk and honey (a picture of a place of blessing). The only problem was that big, powerful and treacherous giants lived in the land, and they had to be eradicated. When Moses sent twelve spies into the land to scope it out, the spies returned with evidence of the land's incredible prosperity, but ten of the twelve spies were scared out of their wits by the size of the giants. Only Joshua and Caleb were convinced that their God was powerful enough to defeat the giants. Ten men said, "It's a hopeless situation; the giants are too big!" And two men said, "The situation is a great opportunity; our God is bigger than the giants." Eventually the ten spies who were overwhelmed by the giants died in the wilderness, and Joshua and Caleb had the privilege and joy of seeing the mighty hand of their Lord defeat the enemy so the Israelites could live in the land of promise.

This Old Testament account is a helpful picture of you and me. Our flesh can be likened to the Promised Land that was occupied by the giants. We have one giant, sin, that has invaded our land. I'd liken our spirit to that of Joshua and Caleb. They had unwavering confidence that the mighty, invincible power of the Lord God could easily defeat the giants. If you read the account of how the Promised Land was claimed, you'll see that it was the mighty, supernatural power of our Lord that defeated the enemy. Joshua and Caleb and the children of Israel went forth, but every step of the way they were claiming victory because their God was exercising his powerful arm that no enemy could resist.

Let the Rubber Meet the Road

I have identified six insights from this study that have changed my thinking and behavior toward sin and my flesh. I have stated them for you in the form of action steps.

1. *Create a picture in your mind of who you are.* I see myself as a person who is inseparably united with a loving heavenly

Father, and I live in a house called *flesh*. Unfortunately a clever, manipulative force called *sin* got to my house before I did and made a mess of it in many ways. I now occupy my house and have found a *power* that will allow me to reclaim my house from the power of sin.

2. *Learn to think and verbalize these two aspects of who you are when you are tempted to sin or after you have sinned.* I often prayerfully say, "Father, sin is exerting its power to make my flesh want to . . . (whatever the sinful action is). My flesh is aching to do it, but I don't want any part of it. You alone are the power that can deal with the power of sin in my flesh." It has been extremely helpful to precisely identify who the culprit is and where he is making his attack. I also find it critical to identify what my flesh is thinking, what it is feeling and what it wants to do, and, in contrast, what I—the real me who is bonded to the Spirit of God—want to do.

A long time ago I kept blurring these two distinctions and came away defeated, thinking that as a child of God I was will-fully participating in what sin was prompting the flesh to accomplish. Then I realized that whenever the voice of sin was prompting my flesh to indulge itself, there was always another quiet voice saying, "This isn't the way. I don't want to dishonor my Lord." I learned to recognize that as the voice of my spirit. Clarifying this distinction was an important step for me in learning how to deal with the enemy within.

Let me give you an analogy that others have found helpful. Perhaps you are one of the many people who own roach-infested homes. It's not that the house is overrun with roaches, but you occasionally see one lurking around. Those disgusting little critters hide in cracks in the walls and sneak out at night to explore the house. Imagine that one day you invite me to spend a couple of days at your house. Before bed, I decide to get a drink of water, so I go to the kitchen, turn on the light and see two roaches nibbling on some crumbs on the counter. My first instinct might be to run back into your living room and say, "You are a dirty, filthy person! You've got roaches in your house. I don't want anything to do with you anymore." You'd protest, "You're confusing my house with me. My house is my dwelling place, but it's not me. Norm, you need to go see a therapist!"

Can you see the parallel? Your flesh is your house that the real you—a spiritual person—lives in. Your house has an infestation of sin, but you are a redeemed, beloved child of God who is learning your Lord's strategy of how to clean up the house. It's interesting that most of us have to get professional help to get rid of roaches. We shouldn't be surprised if we need "professional help" from our Lord to deal with the problem of sin in our house. Don't let your identity be the sin that seeks to exploit your flesh. *You are not your sin.* You are a child of God learning how to find freedom for your house.

3. *Ask yourself, "Do I really believe that there is a power greater than the power of sin in my flesh?"* For a long time I never asked myself that question. Sin had reigned in my flesh for so long, leading me to patterns of defeat, that I had unknowingly come to believe, like the ten spies, that it was a hopeless cause. I thought I'd just have to live with this pattern for the rest of my life. But one day, I backed myself into a corner and said, "Norm, the Bible clearly says that nothing or no one is as powerful as the Lord. Do you believe that he is more powerful than the sin that keeps ravaging your flesh?" At first I answered a meek yes, because I knew that I would be denying the Word of God if I answered otherwise. But gradually the conviction grew within until I could answer with a resounding

"*Yes!* He is greater!" Once I knew that my sovereign Lord was greater than the power of sin in my flesh, I knew that I would not have to be enslaved to it any longer.

4. *Recognize that the Lord doesn't remove sin from your flesh when you are born again.* In my early Christian experience, I'd hear people proclaim a message of entire sanctification that indicated that we should never have a problem with sin once we become a Christian. That messed up my mind when I compared it with my own experience. But I now see that the Scriptures clearly teach that our Lord doesn't choose to remove sin from our flesh when we become a Christian. I believe one reason for this is that we are motivated to grow more when we have to call on his resources to combat this internal enemy.

We mature by coping with the enemy through our Lord's strength. I gave you an analogy earlier about the Israelites and the Promised Land. Our Lord didn't wipe out the enemy and then let the Israelites enter. He let them participate in the cleansing of the land because that process was necessary for their faith to grow. Seeing their Lord at work made him real to them. In the same way, as we call on our mighty Deliverer and see him defeat the enemy, it causes our faith to grow and our admiration of him to soar.

5. *Accept the fact that the battleground is the mind.* That's where the serpent confronted Eve in the garden. He sought to control her thinking, to get her to think about her Lord and herself in an inaccurate way. He still uses that same tactic today. He messes with our mind, knowing that what we come to believe shapes our emotions and our actions. You and I have grown up in a world system that has played games with our minds, and we often don't grasp how much we've come to believe the evil one's manipulation and deceit. Sin fights hard

to control your mind because that is the source that triggers the emotions. And when our emotions are inflamed, we have a hard time saying no to sinful actions. Our emotions don't think; they are much like a spoiled child that throws a tantrum and insists, "I want what I want, and I want it *now!*" The Spirit of God is also seeking access to our minds. Unless we are willing to hear him, we will never learn the truth and invite him to release his mighty power to defeat sin's lie.

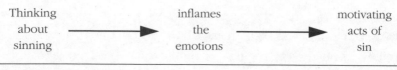

Thinking about sinning ⟶ inflames the emotions ⟶ motivating acts of sin

Figure 2

6. *Recognize that our Lord's purpose is to restore the unity of body and spirit.* He does this by defusing sin's power to direct our flesh to sinful responses. When the flesh comes under the powerful authority of the Spirit of God, it responds consistently with our redeemed spirit. The hope I can share with you is that our loving Lord is committed to restoring the unity between your flesh and your spirit, and he does this by defeating the power of sin in your flesh and bringing the flesh under the authority and care of the Spirit of God.

Making It Personal

1. Study the verses I've shared with you in this chapter and in the endnotes to be clear about the ways the word *flesh* is used in the New Testament.

2. It is crucial that you see the difference between your spirit and your flesh. Review this chapter so that you understand where sin makes its assault and where your power base is for defeating sin's power.

3. What is the danger of saying, "My flesh is evil," rather than saying, "The sin that seeks to rule my flesh is evil"?

4. I've said that the battle is for the mind. What strategy does the Bible teach to purify, strengthen and protect the mind?

8

TAKE ME TO
YOUR LEADER

*"The controversy of the universe
is centered on who shall have the authority."*
WATCHMAN NEE

*"But I say, walk by the Spirit,
and you will not carry out the desire of the flesh."*
GALATIANS 5:16 (NASB)

For ten years my wife and I lived at 7th Place in Phoenix.
Across the street, there were about eight small cottages around
a central house. The cottages were built years ago to be rentals
for people who wintered in Phoenix. During the time we lived
on that street, that property was sold to a new owner I'll call
Max. He told me that a man had approached him and offered
to oversee the property, convincing Max that he would
improve the property and oversee rentals. So the manager
moved in.

In a very short time we saw junk accumulate on the property. Within a year it looked like a scrap yard. Max's efforts to
rescue his deteriorating property were in vain because he
feared the manager. His property was clearly under the control
of the manager, and Max could do nothing about it. What once

had been a lovely property became a frustration to its owner and an eyesore to the neighbors.

One day a higher authority took over. The city ruled that the property was violating zoning laws and sent a cleanup crew to haul away the trash. They boarded up the cottages and made it clear that they must not be occupied. But the manager still lived in the main house. Within a few months he was up to his old tricks and inviting friends to move into the cottages. When the zoning officials found out, the cleanup crew returned, and this time they demolished every building and left the land bare. The manager was evicted. What Max couldn't do, the authority of the city of Phoenix did. I've often thought of Max's dilemma. He didn't have the power to manage his own property. Although he owned it, he couldn't control what went on there.

 Principle #7: Either sin will rule our lives, or the Spirit of God will rule.

The incident I've described raises an important question: Who is my leader? When we become adults, we assume that we've broken free of parental restraints and are cleared to take charge of our own lives, make whatever decisions we want and resolve our own difficulties. We're the captains of our own ships, free to sail any ocean we want and do whatever we choose. This attitude makes us reluctant to admit that we can't understand some issue or solve a certain problem. Many of us don't know where we are going, but we refuse to stop and ask directions! Perhaps this is why many of us resist going to someone like a marriage counselor for help. We've fallen for the lie that we can manage our life quite well without outside direction.

When we address the problem of sin in our lives, we have three leadership options. One, we can surrender to sin and allow it to control the direction of our lives. Since it already has established a foothold in our flesh, we can reluctantly resign ourselves to its manipulation, intimidation and bullying. If we are honest, at sometime in our life we've had to admit, "Sin is in control. It has overpowered me and forced me to submit to its desires. Sin is telling me what to do, and I don't have the power or will to counteract its oppressive rule." We're like Max, wanting something good but receiving something bad from the evil in control.

The second leadership option comes from a thought-provoking quote from a friend of mine. He said, "I've discovered that arrogance is trusting myself with myself." We don't like to think of ourselves as arrogant, but many of us are living self-directed lives. We're dishonest about the level of arrogance we exhibit. The idea of self-leadership is very prominent in our society. We are told that we can solve any personal problem if we set our mind to it. Throughout life, messages like the following are drilled into our heads:

• "Don't give me excuses. Just knuckle down and decide that you're going to resolve the problem."
• "If you really wanted to do something about it, you could."
• "Just bite the bullet and get on with it."
• "You're lazy. Responsible people don't do those things."
• "Grow up! Be a man [woman], and lick that addiction."

Whether consciously or subconsciously, many of us have chosen this self-centered, self-directed way of life.

The other way we get to this point is through a prideful spirit. We find that we have a fine mind, athletic prowess, a knack for making money or a strong personality. I'm sure that Max had felt confident that he would be able to care for his property and keep the manager in line. Unfortunately he found that this wasn't the case. We too deceive ourselves into believing that we are capable of doing anything we choose. Sometimes we're fed a message from others who are bragging on our strengths, and we begin to believe that we are God's gift to humanity. Sometimes this is mixed in with our distrust of anyone else, and we choose to be self-directed. Our thought is, *I'm my own leader. I don't need anyone else.* David Roper describes this thought process in an interesting way:

> It is my pride that makes me think I can call my own shots. That feeling is my basic dishonesty. I can't go it alone. I can't rely on myself. I am dependent on God for my very next breath. It is dishonest of me to pretend that I am anything but a man, small, weak, limited. So living independent of God is self-delusion. It is not just a matter of pride being an unfortunate little trait and humility being an attractive little virtue. It is my inner psychological integrity that is at stake. When I am self-dependent, I am lying to myself about what I am. I am pretending to be God and not man. My independence is the idolatrous worship of myself, the national religion of hell.[1]

The serpent convinced Adam and Eve to follow their own star and become their own leader on that fateful day that ended in disaster. Eve fell for the lie that she would be better off shedding her Lord's leadership to become a free spirit. In truth, she was setting herself up to be enslaved to a new master that would rob her of all the peace, joy and love that she knew under her Sovereign. In the end, both Adam and Eve were swindled out of an invaluable possession.

Option number two is really not an option at all. When we think we are our own bosses, we are playing the part of the fool. We are not capable of being self-directed. We too are being deceived by the evil one. Eve looked into the distorted mirror that the serpent held before her and saw an inde dent woman, successfully carving out her own future w own mind. When she bought the lie, Eve found that she was incapable of pulling off this grand scheme. And we, her off-spring, carry on this grand illusion. I say *illusion* because I don't think most of us are in touch with our arrogant spirit. It is too deeply rooted, too subtle, too innocent looking. We think we are being responsible, but the truth is we are encroaching on our Lord's territory when we try to manage sin in our lives.

Richard Nixon said, "Before we become too arrogant with the most deadly of the seven deadly sins, the sin of pride, let us remember that the two great wars of this century, wars which cost twenty million dead, were fought between Christian nations praying to the same God."[2]

When I was a young Christian, I memorized Proverbs 3:5-6: "Trust in the Lord with all your heart and lean not on your own understanding; in all your ways acknowledge him, and he will make your paths straight." After it was planted in my mind, I began to wonder why I shouldn't lean on my own understanding. My logic went something like this: "Lord, you've given me a fine mind. Why shouldn't I rely on it to solve problems and make a life plan?" What I discovered as I experienced life is that no matter how capable my mind is, it isn't adequate to show me my blind spots. It isn't capable of knowing everything. The longer I've lived, the more I realize how limited my understanding is. It's been freeing to recognize that I need someone greater than myself to bring oversight to my life.

Let's explore a third option. Option three recognizes our need for someone to give positive, healthy leadership in our lives—someone who is trustworthy, someone wiser than we are, someone who is powerful to confront ungodly influences and someone who loves us unconditionally. Someone like our heavenly Father.

Discovering the Great Exchange

In researching this book, I spent hours reading and reflecting on Romans 5—8. As I pored over these chapters, I was struck with the repetition of certain words and phrases that relate to the issue of personal leadership. It's clear that *we will never cope successfully with the problem of sin if we don't have the right leader leading us.* When we looked at the creation account in Genesis, we observed that Adam and Eve were created to be led. They had no personal capacity to cope with the problem of sin. They were created in innocence, not knowing right from wrong, so without someone to lead them they could never resolve the problems that life would throw at them. In fact, they struck out their first time at bat; they never got to first base.

The more I studied Romans, the more I realized that Paul basically presents a three-phase sequence that we must comprehend. In essence it is a process of *exchanged leadership.* The number of verses that support each stage overwhelmed me. My hope is that the sheer number of references will drive home to you the clarity with which Paul demonstrates this process. All Scripture references will be from the New American Standard Bible because I believe the wording is helpful for our study. I've also highlighted certain words for emphasis.

Phase one: Sin controls our lives. A careful reading of Romans 5—7 will reveal a significant number of verses that emphasize how much sin rules over the child of God. When I first saw this, I was impressed by Paul's consistent emphasis. The following four verses (from NASB) are representative:

- "Sin *reigned* in death" (Romans 5:21).
- "Do not let sin *reign* in your mortal body that you should obey its lusts" (Romans 6:12).
- "You were *slaves* of sin" (Romans 6:17).

• "I am of flesh, sold into *bondage* to sin" (Romans 7:14; see appendix A for additional verses).

After I'd reviewed my list of verses, several insights flooded my mind. First, I was struck by the fact that sin is clearly described as an active, powerful force that brings my flesh to its knees to do what sin dictates. There is not the smallest hint that we have the personal power to stand up to this tyrant. Sin has usurped the leadership position over our flesh, hands down, just like Max's manager did to his property. As I pondered this, I wondered how many of us believe it.

In my research, I came across a statement by a Bible scholar who comments on the word *reign*. Paul uses it three times: in Romans 5:21, 6:12 and 6:17. Paul says, "Therefore do not let sin reign in your mortal body so that you obey its evil desires" (Romans 6:12). In his book on Romans, R. C. H. Lenski notes, "The very verb *basileuo* regards 'the sin' as a king who 'reigns.' Now it would be useless to tell sinners not to let this powerful king, sin, reign over them, whether in their mortal bodies or in the rest of their being; sinners could not prevent the sin's reigning over them."[3]

Second, I noticed that sin is described as a power that acts on the members of our physical body. It permeates the body's desires, it infiltrates the mind's thought process, and it gains access to one's emotions. Beginning with my earliest childhood experiences, sin conquered the entirety of my flesh and established leadership authority over it. It was my mentor showing me how to meet my needs in illegitimate ways. These ways became habits that became entrenched in my mind and emotions.

Third, I saw that the words used in the verses I've highlighted stress sin's ability to dictate what the flesh will think, feel and do. These verses don't give the slightest indication that

I am a free, autonomous person living my life as I please. Rather I am under the control of sin; it is the ruling master of my flesh.

Finally, I saw that Paul clearly says that someone must rescue me from sin's enslaving power. I am powerless to do this. Nothing in the text indicates that I am capable of resolving this shameful dilemma. The bottom line is that Paul tells us we are under captive leadership and have no personal power to overthrow this evil dictator. Until we come to complete agreement with Paul's assessment, we will never find freedom from sin's captivity. Only when we give up our illusion that we can bring sin under control by our own efforts will we be ready for our Lord's solution. Beware of anyone who tells you otherwise. If you have any question, reread the list of verses I've posted above.

Phase two: Sin's official power is broken. Paul's epistle to the Romans demonstrates the mighty act our Lord accomplished when Jesus Christ died on the cross. In that monumental event, sin's legal, or legitimate, power over us was broken. Never again will it have free reign over those who have entrusted themselves to God. Paul again documents this reality over and over. Observe in the following verses (from NASB) what our Lord has done that changes our relationship to the evil tyrant, sin:

- "We who *died to* sin . . ." (Romans 6:2).
- "Our old self was crucified with Him, that our body of sin might be done away with, that we should *no longer be slaves to sin*" (Romans 6:6).
- "Sin *shall not be master* over you" (Romans 6:14).
- "Having died to that by which we *were bound . . .*" (Romans 7:6; see appendix B for a complete list of verses).

This second set of verses also produces several helpful insights. They make it crystal clear that our sovereign Lord has dethroned sin's right to dominate our body and soul.

Paul says that an action occurred that stripped sin of any right to claim our flesh as its domain. When we placed our faith in Jesus Christ, we gained a legal basis to reject sin's claim on us. We still have to call upon a Power outside ourselves to enforce the new ruling, but knowing that a ruling has been passed down against sin, and knowing that ruling has teeth in it, should give us encouragement and a firm conviction to stand against sin's efforts. Sin no longer has any legal claim over our flesh. It will continue to act as though it does, but the Bible says that sin's authority over our flesh has been broken. That's a biblical fact.

But our Lord has done more. He did something to us. We died to sin. Our relationship to sin in our flesh has changed. The Bible says that we died to sin, but it doesn't say that *sin died to us*. I hope you can see the implications of this distinction. Our Lord does something in us to break sin's grip, but we have to claim the rights this change provides.

Imagine that someone brings a charge against you in a court of law. At the trial the judge tosses out the charge brought against you. From that point on the person who brought the charge has no legal claim against you, even though he may continue to threaten, harass or accuse you. You could allow yourself to be controlled by that person's domination, but the domination does not have any legal basis. You could just as easily reject the party's false claim and walk away.

Paul stresses that we died to the power that binds our flesh. I hope you notice that the words *body* and *members of our body* are used frequently to distinguish that sin makes its assault on our body rather than our spirit, which is united to the Spirit of God. Our struggle is with a body that craves fulfill-ment, emotions that desire to express themselves in ungodly ways, and a mind that has been programmed to think unhealthy, evil thoughts.

Our Lord has condemned sin. It is on his black list. Its authority has been broken. Our challenge is to believe this with strong conviction and begin to act with authority toward sin. We have a biblical basis to reject sin's false authority over us in the midst of its continued harassment, intimidation and temptation. But we're not done yet. To find freedom we have to move on to phase three.

Phase three: New power for new freedom. Before we came to Jesus Christ, sin had established a ruling authority over our flesh. It acted as king and our flesh bowed as the subject doing what the king demanded. Then Jesus Christ dethroned sin in our flesh. But an empty throne, or no leadership in our life, is dangerous because the old king may try to rule illegitimately. Thus our first course of action is to welcome the new king to the throne. Next, we should stand in the new authority delegated by our heavenly Father. You can, and should, say to sin, "You have no authority over my flesh. I refuse to recognize your rights over my flesh. I recognize a new Sovereign and him alone." Finally, we should call upon the new Power, the Spirit of God, to become the rightful authority over the flesh.

Paul makes it clear that we must embrace the new sovereign leadership if we are ever to experience true freedom. Examine the following verses from the book of Romans. As before, notice the italicized words that clarify the new leadership for our lives. These verses (again from NASB), and the consistent message each sends, should confirm that the intention of our gracious Father is to bring new leadership to our flesh:

• "As sin *reigned* in death, even so grace might *reign* through righteousness to eternal life through Jesus Christ our Lord" (Romans 5:21).

• *"Present yourselves* to God as those alive from the dead, and your members as instruments of righteousness to God" (Romans 6:13).

• "Having been freed from sin, *you became slaves* of righteousness" (Romans 6:18).

• "But now we have been released from the Law, having died to that by which we were bound, so that *we serve* in newness of the Spirit" (Romans 7:6; see appendix C for a complete list).

Now we have come to the core of the issue. A new reigning Power has come to reside in us. This Power is mightier than any other force in the universe. He is mightier than the dethroned enemy, sin. Do you believe this? Unless you believe that there is a Power that can defeat the power of sin in your flesh, you will never find freedom from its dominion. Here are my observations from the verses that I highlighted for you.

One, there is no middle ground regarding the issue of leadership over our lives. It's very clear from Paul's writings that we are not capable to rule our flesh independently. It's not a viable option if we want true freedom. Someone will give direction to our lives. Our options are either that sin rules or that Jesus Christ rules through the indwelling Holy Spirit. And he must have full authority, or we'll never find release from sin's harassment and intimidation. Our Lord has won the battle. The victory is ours to claim, but it can only be claimed if we welcome the new King into our lives, joyfully bow before him and pledge allegiance to him. He has demonstrated over and over that he is a kind, compassionate and gentle Sovereign who wants to bring joy to our lives. But make no mistake, he must be welcomed wholeheartedly and given full authority to lead us. There is no other way to find freedom from sin's control of the flesh. There is no plan B.

Two, as we submit to this new Power within us, it gains access to our flesh—our physical, mental and emotional being—and begins to reclaim it as a clean, purified temple. Our Lord never despises our flesh; he wants to redeem it.

Three, we are not the power that can defeat sin in our flesh, but we are an active participant in the process. Our Lord asks us to join him in standing up to sin's false claim and call upon the new Power, the Spirit of our Lord, to call sin's bluff. This mighty Power not only subdues sin but fills our flesh with God's presence and power. One way we participate in the process is described in Ephesians. We are instructed to "put on the full armor of God so that [we] can take [our] stand against the devil's schemes" (Ephesians 6:11). As we carefully examine the text, we see that the armor is our Lord's mighty, irresistible resources—not our natural strength. As we wear his power and protection, we participate with him.

Four, this is a process that we learn. Perhaps you were like me, looking for a magical key that would immediately set everything right. But our Lord's way is different. He initiates a process that we learn to follow. Like every other process, it takes time and practice to become comfortable with it. Our Lord will be patient to teach us the process, but we have to be serious about rejecting the old authority and submitting to the new. The more comfortable we become with his leadership, the less our flesh will be victimized by sin's infiltration. But if you don't know the sure ground you stand upon, sin will try to convince you that it is not defeated and that the new Power is not really available. Sin will continue to pursue you until you are defeated again.

You might ask, "Why doesn't our Lord just move in, take over and clean house? Why do I have to be an active participant in this process?" But let me question you: Do you think that our Lord wants a bunch of robots that he's programmed to do good? Could we genuinely love him, worship him and enjoy him if he did this? No, he seeks men and women who are powerfully touched by his redeeming love. He wants men and women who discover that he is trustworthy and will honor his promises. He wants men and women who love purity and embrace it as good. He wants men and women who believe in the kingdom of God and want to join this eternal company.

One thing that makes life fulfilling and challenging is the journey from childhood to adulthood. We call this the process of growth and maturity. Our beloved Lord has a similar, magnificent plan for his people. He yearns for them to become mature spiritual beings who know how to live in wisdom, joy and fruitfulness. He has devised a way to nurture us in this growth process. Sin, on the other hand, seeks to destroy us—to rob us of the thrilling life our Lord has planned for us.

My final observation is that we have to decide if we will sell out to this righteous Power and allow him to become the sovereign leader of our lives, or if we will continue to pretend that we can manage on our own and keep him available as a consultant. Our Lord must be the king of our life. Paul uses the same word, *reign*, to describe Christ as our sovereign leader as he did to describe sin as a leader.

As I worked through this chapter, it occurred to me that those of us who live in Western nations have no concept of a ruling king. But in most of recorded history, the king was sovereign. His rule was absolute. People lived under his direction as his subjects. If we live in a democracy in which the people rule, the concept that we should bow before a sovereign is foreign. But when we consider Jesus Christ as the Sovereign who loves us unconditionally, promises to care for us tenderly, and says that his yoke is easy and his burden is light, we realize that we could never have a better leader.

The other day I drove past my old house on 7th Place. I looked across the street and saw three brand new homes that had been built on Max's property. The property had been "born again" with attractive homes and landscaped yards. When a higher authority took over, they got rid of the evil power and allowed a transformation to occur. What Max couldn't do, the city of Phoenix could. It reminded me that what I am powerless to do, the mighty power of a compassionate Father can.

Most of us have had the wrong leadership in our life for such a long time that the idea of a change of leadership seems threatening or uncomfortable. Our flesh keeps telling us that if we let the Spirit of God have sovereign leadership, we'll miss out on something. The truth is that if we don't honor him as our sovereign leader, we'll miss out in a big way. Our Lord Jesus is not a tyrant, but a loving Friend who has amply demonstrated his willingness to sacrifice for us. Love, joy and peace rule his kingdom. The fruit of his reign is delightful beyond description.

Making It Personal

1. Who do you perceive to be the leader of your life? What kind of a leader has that person been?

2. Compare the serpent's temptation of Adam and Eve with the voices that tempt you to reject God's leadership in your life. What do the voices say to you?

3. Are you convinced that sin's authority and power have been broken in your life? If not, reread the verses I've highlighted in this chapter to see if they can help you gain a strong, biblical conviction.

4. Are you afraid of our Lord's complete leadership in your life? Why or why not?

9

A Crash Diet
or a
Lifestyle Change?

*"Don't try to deal with sin, for you are sure to lose.
Deal with Christ; let him deal with your sin
and you are sure to win."*
ARTHUR H. ELFSTRAND

*"The thief comes only to steal and kill and destroy;
I have come that they may have life, and have it to the full."*
JOHN 10:10

All my life I've had to monitor my weight. When I was a child, most people would have politely described me as chubby, except my three older brothers who felt the liberty to come right out and tell me that I was fat. But when I enlisted in the Navy, the boot camp drill instructors were even less diplomatic and quickly turned up the heat by having me scurry around the oval track until the fat melted off my body. Then when I moved into adulthood, I discovered that I was one of those individuals with a generous appetite that caused me to gain a pound here and a pound there. So I'd go on a crash diet and lose enough weight to salve my conscience until my regular eating habits kicked in again and the cycle repeated itself. (Actually I hastened the process because after

I'd lose the weight, I'd reward my accomplishment with a special treat like an ice cream sundae!)

Then I moved into that stage of life when my body metabolism slowed down, and I found that the crash diet approach didn't work any longer. At about the same time, I read several articles that informed me of the same message: crash diets don't work. Convincing evidence told the truth that those on crash diets may lose the weight, but they don't keep it off. Keeping weight in check requires a change of lifestyle. Eating habits have to change. Exercise has to become a regular part of our activities. So about twenty years ago, I adopted a new physical fitness lifestyle change. I modified my eating habits (although I haven't lost my love for food!). And I work out at a fitness center three days a week. The lifestyle change did far more than a crash diet could ever do. My weight remains constant, and my physical energy is much more consistent throughout the day.

The same principle I've described for building and maintaining physical health can be applied to our spiritual health. We become concerned about annoying or downright shameful patterns of sin in our life, so we go on a spiritual crash diet by making a New Year's resolution. I recall an incident that happened to me years ago that illustrates this. When I was in my early twenties, a coworker caught me in a humiliating situation. I made a passionate vow that I would never again do what I'd done. I gutted it out of my life for a while, but my spiritual crash-diet resolution failed me very soon after my vow because I didn't possess the wisdom or power to deal with the core problem. What I needed was a lifestyle change to deal with the dilemma I faced, and I didn't have a clue how to go about it.

In this book, I've attempted to help you discern how sin

operates in your flesh and how our beloved Lord has engi-
neered a foolproof plan for us to become free from its vicious,
enslaving control. But the plan won't work if we take the crash
diet approach and promise, "I'll never do that again," or make
resolutions like, "I'll try harder to resist next time." What our
Lord is after is a more radical lifestyle change, one in which we
approach the problem from a totally new perspective. I believe
that we can identify several characteristics of this lifestyle
change. To help you evaluate where you are and where you
need basic changes, I will raise several questions and help you
think through the lifestyle issue.

*Am I prepared to let the Spirit of God teach me his plan to free
me from sin's rule over my appetites, my emotions and my
thought processes?* The good news is that sin has no authority
to control your flesh. You don't have to be ruled by sinful,
degrading lust—whether it's the lust for power, for another
person's body, for financial security, for food, for entertain-
ment or whatever. I've shown you scriptural passages over and
over again that clearly say that our Lord doesn't want us to be
ruled by this evil tyrant. But we must be willing to learn about
how that deliverance comes and to commit ourselves to follow
our Lord's plan that will lead to a new liberating lifestyle.

*Do I understand the process that leads me to freedom from
sin's control as outlined in the Bible?* I asked a dear friend to
read through my first draft of this book, and his insights were
very helpful. One of his comments helped me see one of the
fallacies we have about coping with the power and persistence
of sin in our flesh. My friend said something like this: "I would
love to see you add more stories of victory over sins like greed,
gluttony, pride, selfishness, independence and anger. . . . People love 'Rocky' stories. Tell them victory stories, and give
more examples to inspire and create hope." My friend's com-

ment prompted much thought. I realized that we all want a victory story that we can hold onto to find hope. But I believe that the answer to the sin problem is not victory—the idea that I've finally licked this once and for all. Sin never lets up its relentless pursuit. And, by the way, that's not bad news. Our Lord is teaching us a new way to live. He leads us through the valley of the shadow of death—not around it. He is teaching us how to live joyfully and successfully while the enemy stands across the street trying to entice, intimidate or bully us.

That concept is very meaningful to me. As I mentioned in the last chapter, I owned a home for years that was across the street from a renter who was a pain in the neck. He trashed the owner's property until the city condemned it and had the structures torn down. Initially I stewed, worried and fumed at the renter's mean spirit and lack of consideration of others. But finally my Lord got through to me and showed me that my joy was not dependent on what my neighbor did. I woke up every morning with a choice. I could focus on his behavior and have a miserable day, or I could focus on my Lord and have joy in the midst of a deteriorating neighborhood. I chose the latter and found that it worked. I learned a process that I acted upon daily. It wasn't victory; it was joy in the midst of problems.

Looking for victory was one of the snares that kept me trapped for many years. I wanted our Lord to deliver me from temptation, sin and shame. I wanted to wake up one day and say, "It's over." That was faulty thinking. Our flesh will have desires until we draw our last breath. Sin will endeavor to whisper its message to the end. But our Lord promises us a way that leads to joy. I finally began to understand that my Lord had a plan to help me grow up spiritually. One essential component of this was to get me on the right track mentally, emotionally and spiritually concerning how the power of sin could really be defused in my life. I found that his plan really works.

Typically a lifestyle change involves a process that we go through, moving from one pattern of thinking, feeling and acting to another. You didn't just decide to drive a car one day and were immediately able do it. You went to the Department of Motor Vehicles and picked up a manual to study the rules of the road. After passing a test that indicated you knew the basic information, you were granted a learner's permit. Then the challenge really began. You had to practice what you'd learned in the learner's manual and demonstrate that you could handle the operation of an automobile or truck. Even after you passed your driver's test, you continued to learn and refine driving skills. Today you probably feel quite comfortable driving. But getting to this place was an involved process.

I'm suggesting that you are learning a new process to live free from sin's tyranny. In a way similar to learning to drive, you need accurate information, practice in applying the information and a growing proficiency to keep doing the necessary things. Usually it is valuable to have someone coaching us through the process. If we don't have an overview of what should happen, we could get confused. Or we may try a part of it but find it doesn't work. Or we may think we're doing something correctly ("If I could keep the Ten Commandments perfectly, I'd stop sinning!"), when that's not even a part of the process. You may want to review the principles I've outlined in earlier chapters to be certain you understand where you are now and where our Lord wants to lead you. It's important that you understand what your responsibilities are and what our Lord's responsibilities are.

What has been my focus in the past? Individuals who are trapped in patterns of sin are usually overly focused on the sins they are committing. This leaves them with an underlying sense of shame, guilt and emptiness. Our Lord wants us to initiate a lifestyle change in which we shift the focus from sin to our Lord. By building and maintaining a healthy, positive relationship with our compassionate Father, we gain new internal strength. Preoccupation with sin causes us to lose sight of the source of our strength, and we then become all the more vulnerable to sin's appeal. So I'm suggesting a fundamental shift of focus.

As I was studying how the apostle Paul viewed this matter, I was impressed with an observation by J. Knox Chamblin: "With respect to his sin, as in other respects, Paul is not preoccupied with himself. He does not often talk about his sins. What evidence we have indicates that Paul is by no means indifferent to his sins. He recognizes their enormity and their tenacity."[1] But while he is honest about them, he is not obsessed with them. He gives no indication that his sins rob him of joy, or undermine his love, care and service to others. "Joined to his self-awareness as a sinner is an astonishing freedom of spirit and zest for work. The explanation lies in his ongoing experience of God's grace and the Spirit's power."[2]

Because Paul maintains this God-centered perspective, he can write to the Philippian Christians, "I want to know Christ and the power of his resurrection and the fellowship of sharing in his sufferings, becoming like him in his death" (Philippians 3:10). He makes clear that he has not yet arrived, but keeps his eyes looking forward. One can hear his determination when he says, "One thing I do: forgetting what is behind and straining toward what is ahead, I press on toward the goal to win the prize for which God has called me heavenward in Christ Jesus" (Philippians 3:13-14).

The Bible is clear that our strength is drawn from our Lord. He alone is sufficient to meet our needs and provide a sense of

peace and joy. It occurred to me one day that people who are
filled with joy and peace have fewer problems with sin. I didn't
say they don't sin. I'm saying that sin exploits empty, unfulfilled lives. Individuals who are filled with joy are not as easily
led into sin. Sin has a more difficult time selling its product
when the customer is already satisfied.

What is my source of power? I want to challenge you to be
completely honest with yourself. Is Jesus Christ *really* the sovereign ruler of your life? Or is he more like a constitutional
monarch who functions more like a figurehead than an actual
ruler. England has a monarch that sits on a throne and wears a
crown for special events, but that person is a cultural symbol
rather than a ruling authority. Other government leaders make
the real decisions. In the same manner, we may be giving Jesus
Christ lip service as our Sovereign, but his actual authority in
our lives may be nil. We sing hymns and praise songs about
how wonderful he is and listen to teachings from the Bible, but
then we go out and live our lives the way we want. This lifestyle will never lead us to victory over sin's domination.

A long time ago I made an important discovery: My problem
with sin is directly related to my view of and intimacy with my
heavenly Father. Perhaps your most pressing need is to discover who he really is and how deeply he cares for you. When
we see our Lord as an adversary who is waiting to pounce on
us or as a celestial grouch, we don't gain any strength or
encouragement to cope with the problem of sin. But when we
see him as our most compassionate encourager, we find that
sin becomes less attractive and less powerful in our flesh. I
don't have the space in this book to adequately explore how
you develop an intimate relationship with our Beloved, but I
encourage you to nurture that life-changing connection.

The lifestyle change we need is one that teaches us how to

draw upon the ultimate source of power for life. We've seen that sin was the ruling power before we came to faith in Jesus Christ. But sadly many Christians continue under this illegitimate power and experience constant frustration, defeat and discouragement. Or we foolishly stumble along, believing that we can live our lives on our own strength and knowledge. Until we understand that we have been linked to the ultimate power for life, we will be trying to cope with sin in our own feeble, inadequate strength. Learning to walk in partnership with this mighty Power is one of the key components to this new lifestyle.

What are the characteristics of my thought life? The battle is for the mind because whoever controls our minds will control our emotions, and this in turn motivates our actions. Sin gained the upper hand, in that it had the first chance to infiltrate my mind and shape my thinking before I knew Christ. This truth hit me many years ago when I realized that whenever I went to take a shower, my mind began to think in a certain way without my being conscious of it. So sin had established *patterns of thinking* that could leap into action with the slightest trigger or provocation. We use the phrase "pushing my buttons" to describe an incident in which someone's word or glance triggers a reaction within us. Our response can be lightning fast—so quick that we are not even aware of thinking about it. That's how sin operates.

Our Lord is endeavoring to change our thought processes. He wants us to learn how to think differently as a way of life. To do this, we have to grant him the authority to guide our thinking process into new, healthier patterns. Paul demonstrates this principle in his letter to the Romans. He appeals to them, "Do not conform any longer to the pattern of this world, but be transformed by the renewing of your mind. Then you will be able to test and approve what God's will is—his good, pleasing and perfect will" (Romans 12:2). The lifestyle change is spoken of in three stages. One, I reject the pattern of thinking common to a godless society—that which we have been schooled in for many years. Two, I present my mind to my Lord for his transformation. And three, I begin to test and approve his way of thinking, feeling and acting, and I let this become my way of life. While I can outline these steps cleanly and concisely, the process of transformation takes much longer. This is true because the old patterns of thinking have been skillfully woven into the fabric of our thought processes, and we must discover our Lord's truth and allow the Spirit of God to root out the false and plant the new way of thinking in our mind. The sooner we submit to this process, the sooner we'll notice sin's power diminishing.

Paul reminds us that our thinking is controlled from one of two sources. In writing to the Roman Christians, he said that when sin is given free reign in the mind, it will inflame the emotions to acts of sin. But when the Spirit of God is given unlimited access to our mind, we will begin to experience a lifestyle of life and peace (Romans 8:5-6).

I've developed two habits that help me cooperate with what the Spirit of God is trying to accomplish in me. One, I've pre-packaged my thinking. What I mean is that I've taken specific verses from the Bible and committed them to my memory so that they are readily available whenever sin tries to slip unhealthy thinking into my mind.

For example, I mentioned earlier that at one time sin had programmed me to think that my kind and compassionate heavenly Father was always disgusted with me. Whatever I did would not satisfy him. I began to recognize that it was a lie, but I didn't know how to renew my mind. Then I read Psalm 145:8: "The Lord is gracious and compassionate, slow to anger and rich in love." From that point on, whenever the faulty thinking sprung up in my mind, I'd allow the Spirit of God to remind me that the truth was Psalm 145:8. My part was to agree with the new truth being planted in my mind. And with patience on my part, it began to take root, pushing out the old way of thinking.

A second habit I've developed is to catch the sin-produced thoughts earlier and acknowledge their source. I was having coffee with a friend earlier this week. He told me about the way he was threatening and belittling his children. Then he said, "Norm, about halfway through this episode, it suddenly occurred to me that I was acting out fear that was in my heart. I realized that my unhealthy thinking and emotional outburst was being prompted by sin." Afterward we talked about learning how to catch that pattern earlier so that my friend could allow the Spirit of God to direct his thinking and protect his emotions and actions. It is not difficult to catch unhealthy thinking earlier and earlier so that it doesn't get the opportunity to run wild and create havoc within others and us.

Do I recognize the conditions in which sin thrives in my life? The more I examined sin's subtle strategy to bring me to my knees, the more amazed I became at how ignorant I had been of its insidious infiltration in my life. I began to realize that sin thrives in certain situations—even situations that I thought would increase my resistance to sin's control. For example, *sin thrives under law.* Our natural tendency is to think that law would restrain sin. But Paul tells us that it has the opposite effect. He notes, "But sin took advantage of this law and aroused all kinds of forbidden desires within me!" (Romans 7:8 NLT). Well-meaning Christian leaders believe that the establishment of rules and prohibitions will keep people from sinning. Paul would say to them, "That won't work. It will stimulate the desires more than ever. Something greater has to happen to deal with the problem of sin."

We also know that *sin thrives in secrecy.* And what is our natural tendency? We hide our sin, fearing the condemnation and ridicule of others. But sadly, hiding sin only allows it to grow stronger. When a church family is an environment of grace and safety, individuals are more likely to become transparent about their personal struggles. When there is openness, sin loses its power to manipulate and control us. During my teenage years, I struggled with sexual lust, insecurity and doubts about my salvation. I wanted to find help, but I was scared to death to tell anyone in my church because I feared that I'd be condemned and told to leave. The very place that should have been a place of refuge was the place of fear, causing me to feel that I'd be attacked. So I hid my sin and unwittingly encouraged its growth.

Sin thrives where guilt, shame and worthlessness are stressed. Recently a man told me, "I wish we didn't get so beaten up from the pulpit on Sundays. The preacher seems more committed to emphasize how bad we are, how much we are failing and how unworthy we are than how precious we are to our Lord." The man was a very earnest Christian committed to honoring our Lord. He recognized that when the message constantly exploits our failure, we will not find the help to remedy it. My own experience has been that when God's people are shown how to take positive steps, the majority of them are willing to begin the journey.

Do I cultivate healthy relationships? "Blessed is the man who does not walk in the counsel of the wicked or stand in the way of sinners or sit in the seat of mockers" (Psalm 1:1). It intrigues me that this first psalm begins by stressing the importance of avoiding unhealthy relationships. We are cautioned against allowing evil people to gain access to our lives. The psalm also demonstrates the lifestyle change that I've outlined in this chapter, because after warning against unhealthy relationships, the writer follows by saying, "But his delight is in the law of the LORD, and on his law he meditates day and night" (Psalm 1:2). The basis for this relationship is established by godly authority.

There is a joke about a man who makes an appointment to see his doctor. When he enters the examining room, the physician greets him and asks, "What's the problem? How can I help you?" The patient replies, "Doctor, I've broken my arm in two places."

The doctor's response is, "Well then, stay out of them places!" Though we chuckle at the doctor's counsel, we often get into trouble because we don't know enough to "stay out of them places!" Most of us can identify people and places that trigger thoughts and emotions that can easily lead us to sinful actions.

When my oldest daughter, Amy, attended junior high school, she had a circle of friends that she enjoyed. But when they entered high school, these same students began to adopt a lifestyle that was prompted by sinful desires. Amy faced a choice: Do I run with my friends who now are pursuing unhealthy attitudes and behavior, or do I change friends? I was extremely grateful for my daughter's wisdom to see that it was better for her to find new friends. Maintaining habits of godly character became more important than immoral partying. I believe that decision shaped her entire high school experience and set her on a course that our Lord could bless.

What kind of friends help us to establish a lifestyle in which the Spirit of God can free us from sin's oppression of our flesh? I would suggest that we seek out friends who are committed to live with integrity. When those who influence us are pursuing purity and godly lifestyles, they can encourage us and we can encourage them.

We are wise to seek out individuals with whom we can be transparent and vulnerable. I've mentioned that I'm connected to a group of men who meet regularly to affirm, encourage and challenge each other. It's a safe environment in which each of us can speak openly about the life issues that we are facing and know that we will be heard, respected and supported in our desire to live free from sin's control. In this environment of openness and honesty, sin has little opportunity to remain hidden. These men have become very dear to me. I take their issues seriously, and they take mine in the same spirit.

I believe that it is also important to seek friends who understand how sin operates within our flesh and understand the process our Lord uses to set us free from its clutches. This might mean that you form a study group to work through a book like this one so that each person has a working idea of what the Bible teaches about sin and how to create an environment of grace, safety and mutual support. It's amazing what happens when we put our issues on the table with others who are also committed to grow into men and women of God and then study, pray and advance together.

Making It Personal

1. Review the questions I've raised in this chapter. How do you typically answer the questions?

2. I suggest that you leaf back through the book and identify the key ideas that you want to review, think about more carefully or act upon in your life.

3. I've emphasized that coming to grips with the problem of

sin is a process. Do you understand the process? What stage of the process are you in?

4. Sharing what we are learning is often a helpful way to make it more meaningful to ourselves, and it invites others to learn with us. Who would profit from what you have learned in this book?

APPENDIX A

Verses That Show
How Sin Controls Our Lifes

All from NASB:

Romans 6:6, "that we should no longer be *slaves* to sin."

Romans 6:14, "For sin shall not be *master* over you."

Romans 6:16, "When you present yourselves to someone as *slaves* . . ."

Romans 6:19, "You presented your members as *slaves* to impurity and to lawlessness."

Romans 6:20, "When you were *slaves* of sin . . ."

Romans 6:22, "Now having been *freed from* sin . . ."

Romans 7:18, "The wishing is present in me, but the doing of the good is not."

Romans 7:23, "I see a different law in the members of my body, *waging war against* the law of my mind, and *making me a prisoner* of the law of sin which is in my members.*"

Romans 7:24, "Who will *set me free* from the body of this death?"

APPENDIX B

Verses That Reveal How Sin's Official Power Is Broken

All from NASB:

Romans 6:7, "He who has died is *freed from* sin."

Romans 6:11, "Consider yourselves to be *dead to* sin."

Romans 6:12, "*Do not let sin reign* in your mortal body that you should obey its lust."

Romans 6:18, "having been *freed from* sin . . ."

Romans 7:24, "Who will *set me free* from the body of this death?"

Romans 8:2, "The law of the Spirit of life in Christ Jesus *has set you free from* the law of sin and of death."

Romans 8:3, "*He condemned* sin in the flesh."

APPENDIX C

Verses on Finding
New Power for New Freedom

All from NASB:

Romans 6:4, "in order that as Christ was raised from the dead through the glory of the Father, so *we too might walk in newness of life.*"

Romans 6:11, "Consider yourselves to be *dead to* sin, but *alive to* God in Christ Jesus."

Romans 6:19, "Present your members as slaves to righteousness."

Romans 6:22, "now having been *freed from* sin and *enslaved to* God . . ."

Romans 7:4, "You also were made to die to the Law through the body of Christ, that you might be *joined to another.*"

Romans 7:24-25, "Who will set me free from the body of this death? Thanks be to God *through Jesus Christ our Lord.*"

Romans 8:2, "The law of the Spirit of life in Christ Jesus has set you free from the law of sin and of death."

Romans 8:4, "who do not walk according to the flesh, but according to the Spirit."

Romans 8:6, "The mind set on the flesh is death, but the mind set on the Spirit is life and peace."

NOTES

Introduction
[1]Jim Burna and Greg McKinnon, *Illustrations, Stories and Quotes* (Ventura, Calif.: Gospel Light, 1997), p. 135.

Chapter 2: Deceit, Distortion & Doom
[1]Oswald Chambers, *God's Workmanship* (Fort Washington, Penn.: Christian Literature Crusade, 1960), p. 75.
[2]Steve Bender, "Beauty and Beast," *Southern Living* (April 2000): 100.
[3]David Roper, *Psalm 23: The Song of a Passionate Heart: Hope and Rest from the Shepherd* (Grand Rapids, Mich.: Discovery House, 1994), p. 122.

Chapter 3: The Original Gene Therapy
[1]Ray Stedman, *From Guilt to Glory* (Waco, Tex.: Word, 1978), p. 155.

Chapter 4: My Sin—His Grace
[1]Kenneth Wuest, *Wuest's Word Studies* (Grand Rapids, Mich.: Eerdmans, 1973), 1:89.
[2]Ray Stedman, *From Guilt to Glory* (Waco, Tex.: Word, 1978), 1:135.
[3]Robert J. Morgan, ed., *Nelson's Complete Book of Stories, Illustrations, & Quotes: Ultimate Contemporary Resource for Speakers* (Nashville: Thomas Nelson, 2000), p. 589.

Chapter 5: Living in No Man's Land

[1]Kenneth Wuest, *Wuest's Word Studies* (Grand Rapids, Mich.: Eerdmans, 1973), 1:67.

[2]R. C. H. Lenski, *The Interpretation of St. Paul's Epistle to the Romans* (Minneapolis: Augsburg, 1936), p. 408, italics added.

Chapter 6: Coping with a Home Invader

[1]W. E. Vine, Merrill F. Unger and William White Jr., *Vine's Expository Dictionary of Biblical Words* (Nashville: Thomas Nelson, 1985), p. 576.

[2]Penelope Wilcock, *The Wounds of God* (Wheaton, Ill.: Crossway, 1991), p. 94.

[3]Ibid.

[4]Patti Davis, "Dope: A Love Story," *Time* 7 (May 2001): 49.

Chapter 7: Help! I've Got a Split Personality

[1]Laurence J. Peter, *Peter's Quotations* (New York: Bantam, 1977), p. 285.

[2]Unfortunately the NIV translates the word as "sinful nature." I find this to be a misleading term that confuses how our Lord deals with indwelling sin and fosters the idea of an "old nature" and a "new nature."

[3]Other references include Romans 1:3; 6:19; 9:3, 5, 8; 11:14; 1 Corinthians 6:16; 7:28; 15:50; 2 Corinthians 4:11; 5:16; 7:1; 12:7; Galatians 2:20; 4:13-14; Ephesians 2:11, 15; 5:29-31; Philippians 1:22, 24; Colossians 1:22, 24; 2:1, 5, 13; 3:22; 1 Timothy 3:16; Philemon 16.

[4]Other references include Romans 3:20; 4:1; 8:3; 1 Corinthians 10:18; 2 Corinthians 1:17; 7:5; 10:2-3; 11:18; Galatians 2:16; 3:3; 6:12-13; Ephesians 2:11; 6:5, 12; Philippians 3:3-4; Colossians 2:23.

[5]Other references include Romans 7:25; 8:5-9, 12-13; 13:14; 1 Corinthians 5:5; Galatians 4:23, 29; 5:13, 16-17, 19, 24; 6:8; Ephesians 2:3; Colossians 2:11, 18.

Chapter 8: Take Me to Your Leader

[1]David Roper, *Psalm 23: The Song of a Passionate Heart: Hope and*

Rest from the Shepherd (Grand Rapids, Mich.: Discovery House, 1994), pp. 112-13.

[2]Sherwood Wirt and Kersten Beckstrom, eds., *Topical Encyclopedia of Living Quotations* (Minneapolis: Bethany House, 1982), p. 188.

[3]R. C. H. Lenski, *The Interpretation of St. Paul's Epistle to the Romans* (Minneapolis: Augsburg, 1961), p. 411.

Chapter 9: A Crash Diet or a Lifestyle Change?

[1]J. Knox Chamblin, *Paul and the Self* (Grand Rapids, Mich.: Baker, 1993), p. 25.

[2]Ibid., p. 26.

If you wish to contact Dr. Norm Wakefield with questions, comments or further inquiry, you may do so through <www.Nappaland.com>.